Bouncing Back

Joe —

I hope this Book inspires you to Bounce Back

Brett

Bouncing Back

RECREATE YOUR LIFE

Beth M Whitman

To contact the author, visit
http://www.bouncingback.biz

ISBN Number: 1517210038
ISBN 13: 9781517210038
Library of Congress Control Number: 2015916620
CreateSpace Independent Publishing Platform
North Charleston, South Carolina

Printed in the United States of America

Table of Contents

Dedication

This book is dedicated to the people I loved very much whom I lost much to early.

To my Mom who was always there for me and my family. Her life revolved around taking care of everyone else. She taught me so many things -- from cooking to saving money with coupons. Mom was the glue of our family who was always inviting cousins, aunts, and uncles to our home.

To my Dad who taught me how to be an honest business woman. I received a great passion for baseball and music from my Dad. I also learned a great deal about generosity. He always helped people out whether they were his employees, family or people in the community.

To my late husband Steve. I loved the passion that he gave to his work in music, education, and his youth group kids. He died way too young at the age of 45. He was just starting to find his place in the world.

To my Aunt Polly. She was my role model for women in the work force. I learned a great deal from her from her love of art, music and especially travel. Through my relationship with my Aunt, I was inspired to help people overcome challenges and gain their life back.

Acknowledgements

To MY HUSBAND MIKE. FOR giving me inspiration and love throughout the process of my transformation. Without his support I would probably still be floundering looking for yet another unfulfilling job.

I would also like to acknowledge my sisters who have been with me throughout my life and have pushed me to achieve. Throughout the process of dealing with all the losses in our family, Debra, Hope, and I have stayed close and worked hard to make sure to keep what I call "Shalom Bayit": Peace in the House. Whenever we disagreed, we always knew that keeping our bond as sisters together was more important than the end result.

I would also like to thank Tom and Barbara Ingrassia who have given me the motivation to write my own book. When I read Tom's book *One Door Closes: Overcoming Adversity by Following Your Dreams.* I was so inspired that I felt the desire to write my own book. His wife Barbara has been an amazing help in editing my book.

Introduction

I DECIDED TO WRITE *BOUNCING Back* one day when I was doing a practice health consultation with a fellow student from Institute for Integrative Nutrition. We were giving our backgrounds and I started telling about my losses, but more inspiring to her was how I learned from each loss and moved on and created a new life for myself.

I first thought I would write this book in sections. The first section would be about the major losses in my life. The next section would be about how I made it through, and the final section would be like a workbook for people to learn how to apply lessons. The more I thought about it, the more I realized that my story was one of short significant chapters of "life lessons". To try to force my life into a neat package of three sections of the book just didn't work.

I wrote this book not to just tell my story. I wrote it to inspire others to start their lives over. You can re-create your life. Just living your days without new excitement and joy is unfulfilling.

I created my Bouncing Back practice to work with individuals who have dealt with a loss or a set back and to give them the tools to recreate their lives -- rich with love, purpose and meaning.

CHAPTER 1

Delly Line One

Mom and Dad at my wedding to Steve, May 1991

WHEN I WAS BORN MY Dad said to my Grandfather, "Pa, another girl!" My Grandfather's reply "Check again!" As the third girl, I lived with hand-me downs, shared bedrooms and left-overs. I never felt really special until my sisters both graduated from high school and moved out of the house. Finally, I not only had my own room but had my parents to myself!

I loved spending time with my Mom. One of my favorite things was going to the supermarket with her. I used to love when there was an announcement on the PA that said "Deli Line One." I used to say "Mom, get the phone, they're calling you. " My Mom's name was Adele, but her friends and family called her Delly for short.

I remember in college I called her up to tell her about the good grades I got on my last exams. She was happy for that, but when I told her that I saved $14 with coupons at Price Chopper, she was ecstatic. "That is terrific. How did you save that much? Was it double coupons?" In actuality, it was probably better to learn how to save money at the grocery store than to get an A on an exam. But that was my Mom. Always excited about a great sale.

I wouldn't call her a shopaholic. She was a sale-a-holic. She loved finding sales on things. Even if she didn't need it, she had to buy it. Whenever we visited the house, she always tried to pawn something off on us. "Beth, I found a great deal on this sweater." Even if I had twenty sweaters in that color, she HAD to buy it because it was not only on sale but she had a coupon on top!

I remember going to Dillard's with her in Florida. They had a sale on dresses 70% off. I found five that were great. I didn't need them, but they were screaming to us to buy them. I didn't have any room in my suitcase and they were all for the summer. No problem. My Mom would say "I'll pack them in the car and you can get them when we come home in April." That was my experience with Mom. She loved buying stuff for us (especially if it was on sale!)

Mom was always the person in the Mascott family who kept the family together. Our house was always the place for all the Jewish holidays, Thanksgiving, Hanukah and any time that any cousins or aunts and uncles came to visit. One of my fondest memories of growing up is our family barbeques. My Dad made the barbeque on the old Webber charcoal grill. He wanted it authentic; he would stay there for hours grilling. My Mom kept on coming out with more food, "The coals are still going I have more things from the freezer that I could make."

I remember having my parents for a barbeque at our house. I was very nervous. First, we called my Mom "Mrs. White" She was very neat and my Dad and I would joke that she would take the white glove out and check for dust in my house. Steve and I made a ton of different things for the barbeque, and then my Mom arrived with with a styrofoam cooler. She said, "I figured while the coals were hot we could make these." What she forgot was that we had a gas grill! Anyway she was so impressed that we made everything so fast and it came out delicious.

One time Steve and I hosted Thanksgiving at our house. We watched the Butterball video to make sure the turkey would come out perfect. It did! My Mom was practically in tears. She said, "I have made turkeys for decades and never was it this juicy." She was always afraid that it wouldn't be cooked enough, so we always had very dry chicken or turkey over the years.

Speaking of afraid….. My Mom was always afraid to take chances. I definitely got that from my Mom. My parents had a routine, and if they stuck with that, they were fine. Trying something new was very difficult. I know that moving to Florida was a very hard decision for them. First, they didn't have any real hobbies. My Mom wasn't shy but she had he good friends for years and my Dad was the socializer. In Florida they created their own routine: they went down to the pool, went to Publix's for grocery shopping, and spent time with Bob (my father's twin.)

On December 7, 2006, I talked with my Mom in the morning to go over the plans to drive their car to Florida. Steve and I were going to drive their car to Sarasota to visit Steve's parents and then we would drive across the state to deliver their car to Palm Beach. We would stay a few days with them and then fly home. So that morning, I talked with my Mom about all the details, and she was most excited that I had completed all the logistics for the trip down. I remember shortening the conversation by saying "Mom I have to go. I'm running late to the gym."

Later that afternoon, I got a call from my parents' phone number. With caller ID, I would screen calls when I had more important things to do. In this case, watching the beloved Patriots. So when the phone rang in the middle of the game, I was surprised because I had just talked with my Mom earlier, and they knew the cardinal rule not to call during a game.

I let the phone go to voice mail, but two minutes later the phone rang again. I answered it this time. Instead of hearing my Mom or Dad's voice it was one of their neighbors. She said I needed to drive home right away because my Mom had fallen in the garage. She didn't give any other details.

I grabbed my pocketbook and my keys and ran out the door. I was still wearing my gym clothes, but I didn't even care. I don't even remember driving there. When I arrived, I saw my Dad looking totally in a fog, and my parents' neighbors still in the house. They both told me to drive to the hospital right away. They gave me no details, but just said that my Dad would be over later with my brother-in-law Alan.

I got to the E.R. at Lawrence General Hospital expecting to see my Mom in one of the rooms attached to wires and tubes. Instead, I was ushered into a small room; my sister Hope was there with the Rabbi from my parents' Temple. He looked at me and said "I'm sorry Beth, but your Mom has passed. I just stared at him and my sister; I was so confused. Passed? She just fell in the garage. She was the healthy one. She was only 74 years old.

He told us that she had had a heart attack and fell in the garage. Our father called our neighbor who is a cardiologist, and he immediately called 911. They tried to resuscitate her, but it was too late. She died before they got to the hospital.

My other sister Debra and my Dad came to the hospital and we all went into my Mom's room. It looked like she was sleeping. It was so surreal; I just couldn't believe what was going on.

We finally drove back to my parents' house. We started making phone calls to family and friends. We were all in a daze, not knowing what we had to do and say at this point. My Dad was completely out of it. He looked like a rudderless boat just riding in circles on the lake.

I decided that I would stay with Dad at the house. I had Steve bring me some clothes from home so I would be all set for the next day. I couldn't sleep at all. I kept on seeing her lifeless body, my father's confused face, and my sisters' tear filled eyes.

That morning my sisters came over early and we drove over to the Temple; the Rabbi went over the logistics for both the service and Shiva (mourning period). He kept saying it was our job now to take care of Dad. We had just lost our Mother and he is talking about our job to help Dad? How do we grieve and take care of Dad? We helped create the service, and we filled the Rabbi with stories of our Mom. Debra decided to write the eulogy as well.

We drove to the funeral home. It was surreal; we didn't know what we were supposed to do. The funeral director helped us write the obituary and we sorted out all the details of the day. Picking out a casket made it real; it physically told us that this was it.

I don't even remember the rest of the day. Somehow the next morning we got up and went to the Temple. There were a lot of people there. Not only our family and their friends, but my sisters' and my friends as well. Before the service, we sat in a small room to "greet people." It was really comforting to have so many people there. Everyone was in amazement that she had died so young.

The service was beautiful, and Debra's eulogy was amazing. I couldn't believe how composed she was. She had a lot of cute stories about Mom and her little quirks. After the service, we went to Beth El Cemetery in Chelmsford and then did Shiva at their house. We had decided to have Shiva for two days. This was the beginning of many discussions with my sisters; we disagreed on the details but finally came out with a solution that worked for most of us.

Debra wanted to do Shiva on one day; she didn't see the point of having to go through it for two days. She felt that no one would come the second day. Hope and I knew that there were a lot of people who wouldn't make it if it was only on one day. We were right; there were a lot of people there both days. Somehow my Dad was able to make it through it all.

The big question was "How do we deal with Dad?" He and my Mom were married for just over 50 years. My Mom did everything for him. After my Dad retired, he pretty much stayed at home; they did things together if my Mom initiated it. They went down to Florida not because they particularly loved it, but because they hated the winters in Massachusetts. I also think they did it because my Dad's twin brother did it -- so they did as well.

Now that my Mom was gone, what would he do? They had planned to leave for Florida in a couple of days. That wasn't going to happen. My father was having fainting spells. We had no idea what was going on with him.

Since it was December and my work slowed down with the holiday break, my sisters and I decided that I would stay with Dad during the week, and my sisters would stay on weekends until the end of the year. I could do work from our parents' house since they had a computer and Internet service. At that point, I didn't care if I missed work. I was glad I could spend time with my Dad.

CHAPTER 2

It's All about Dad

Dad and I at a cousin's Bar Mitzvah - 2010

DURING DECEMBER I SPENT THE majority of the month staying with my Dad at his house. I was lucky that working as a director of a student organization gave me two weeks off for holiday break, so I really didn't lose any time. I was able to work from Dad's house and drove home on weekends for my sisters to take over.

During that time Dad and I bonded – whether it was playing cribbage or poker or testing out my cooking skills, we had plenty of time together. What I did notice was that Dad had been going downhill health-wise since Mom died. The other way of looking at it "Was he declining or did Mom hide his deterioration from us? "

I went to a lot of doctors' appointments and got to know his prescriptions, ailments, and doctors better than my own. I remember going to my own doctor one time and she asked me for a list of medications that I was taking. I started listing them off and realized that it was my Dad's medications. The doctor said "I didn't realize that you had so many ailments." I proceeded to tell her, "I'm sorry, those are my Dad's. I am so used to filling out his paperwork that it's second nature! I only take a multi-vitamin".

During that time we learned a lot about assisted living options, home health care agencies and selling homes. It was so overwhelming for my sisters and me. We had no idea where to turn to get the best advice.

Thankfully one of my sisters had a few connections and found a home health aide to stay with Dad during the day and another one for the night. It was a huge burden off our shoulders, but we knew that it was just a short term solution. Dealing with Dad was a full time job for all of us. Back at work, I would get calls from him or a helper about some "emergency"; we became very familiar with Lawrence General Hospital.

Living at the house was too much for Dad, and he needed to be with more people. My sisters and I visited a few facilities and took my Dad to one in

Andover that seemed promising; my family had lived there for over 30 years and my sister lived a few miles down the road. While waiting at the elevator to leave, he collapsed. My sisters were already downstairs (they had taken the stairs) and wondered what had happened to us. They came up and saw an EMT checking his vitals. I was sure that the incident would discourage him from thinking of that assisted living facility; luckily he was fine after he had something to drink and rested for a while. We were also lucky that they didn't have to take him to the hospital.

It was difficult to move him there -- not just logistically, but also emotionally. There goes his independence. No turning back; we needed to sell the home. For weeks and months we worked on packing the house and getting it ready to sell. We had our ideas of what we needed to get done.

In retrospect, we should have hired a stager or worked with Dad's real estate agent so we didn't spin our wheels. It was hard working on some rooms. I remember discovering lists from my Mom of holiday cards she had sent out. She kept everything! Cleaning out her closet was amazing. She had over a dozen black skirts in various sizes and lengths. We also found hundreds of pictures. Since I love taking pictures, I took all the photo albums to my house. It also meant we had to clean out our own old closets, the garage and basement. When we finally felt ready, we called our old neighbor who is a real estate broker. She advised us to rip out all the old carpets because she saw that under the old shag rugs were beautiful hard wood floors. After the floors were refinished, the place looked amazing.

We put the house on the market; they showed it, and within the week we had three offers. Finally, one young couple decided to buy. They were both working in the shoe business. A definite match since my Dad was in the shoe business all of his life. At the closing, my Dad was melancholy but was definitely glad they were buying his house.

Over the years, my Dad adjusted to living at the assisted living facility. He went there using a walker but progressively walked less and less. He was falling and having more trouble getting around the facility. He made several trips to the hospital. Through it all, my Dad kept his sense of humor. He would always flirt with the nurses and joke with the young doctors. He would talk with the aides at his facility about the latest Red Sox or Patriots game.

I remember visiting him at the hospital after his hip operation. He looked more exhausted than usual. I asked him what was the matter and he replied, "Those bums lost it in the 13th inning." The Red Sox were on the West Coast and he had stayed up to watch the entire game.

I got my passion for the Red Sox through my Dad. He had season tickets when I was young. I know the line-up from the mid-seventies better than the current players.

I loved going to the game with him; it was our special time. We would buy peanuts and Fenway Franks. Dad was so into baseball that he would watch the game the next morning or the re-runs from the Red Sox Classic games to keep him busy.

After the Red Sox season ended, my Dad was depressed. It was such a big part of his day that he felt abandoned by the "Boys of Summer."

While I was working at Northeastern University, they had a big event to commemorate the 100th anniversary of the first World Series, which had been played at Huntington Field at Northeastern. (Before Fenway Park was opened) There was an email to faculty and staff inviting participation in a panel about baseball. As an avid fan, I decided to submit a proposal. I was chosen and was one of six panelists to speak-- and the only female. I talked about *Spirituality and Baseball*.

It was a huge honor to be part of the event. It was in 2003 and the Red Sox were in the hunt to win. I remember I was at a Jewish conference and met a reporter from the *Boston Globe*. He was the Spirituality editor. I told him about my speech and he decided to interview me. The editor put a three quarter page article on page two of the *Globe* a few days before Yom Kippur. Everyone at my temple told my parents "I saw Beth in the *Globe*."

In the picture, I was wearing my Red Sox cap (in Hebrew) with a tallis (prayer shall) and my Johnny Damon tee shirt #18 (signifying life in Hebrew)

The speech went extremely well and it brought new fame to my life. I received a call from an advertising firm in the spring of 2004 to be part of a group of clergy to say a prayer for the Red Sox. They were promoting the "Dancing Deer Cookie Company." We were invited to share a prayer on the day before opening day at the entrance of Fenway Park. It was also the day before Passover. I remember saying "I will break the curse of the Bambino but I will not break Passover!"

That summer I received a call from the *Hallmark Channel*. They *googled* "baseball and women" and found my name. They were intrigued by my participation in the panel and the prayer at Fenway Park. They interviewed me at the ballpark of the Lowell Spinners, a minor league affiliate of the Boston Red Sox. I talked about the significance of numbers and baseball, the father/child relationship, and other religious icons in the game.

The best part of the day was when my parents met me at the ballpark and we got to see the game together. The Hallmark Channel videotaped the whole day, but after editing, they used only 5-6 minutes. They aired the segment on Rosh Hashanah. It was a bit ironic because I was speaking about spirituality and baseball and they showed it on the most religious Jewish holiday.

When the Red Sox made it to the playoffs in 2004 against the Yankees and were down 0-3, the original clergy who had said a prayer for the Red Sox at the beginning of the season were asked to come back to Fenway Park again. This time Mayor Menino was there in addition to a few news stations. I made the analogy that the Israelites were wandering in the desert for 40 years, but the Red Sox had been wandering since 1908!

Well our prayer worked. The Red Sox won the World Series that year. We all felt like the Messiah had arrived! My Dad was so proud to wear the World Series championship tee shirt and cap!

CHAPTER 3

Warning Signs

Steve and Wally the Green Monster – February 2009

OVER THE YEARS, MY HUSBAND Steve progressively gained more and more weight. When Steve and I met, he was going to a nutritionist and was losing weight. For our wedding in 1991 he had lost a total of fifty pounds.

I knew weight was an issue because he never exercised, and when he tried it was always a struggle. He also lost the weight for the wedding but not for the long term. He looked great in the pictures, but as soon as we were on our honeymoon, all the diets were off. He gained seven pounds just that week. He always said to not worry about it, but I did. My Dad was big all of his life and it took its toll.

Every year he would start a diet, then get frustrated or derailed, and gain the weight back and more. A lot of it was due to depression. He was always in between jobs or school. With no set schedule, he always felt it was too hard to stick with a diet. He always felt "not good enough" comparing himself to his younger brother or believing that he had never lived up to his father's expectations.

When I first met Steve, he was interested in becoming a cantor. He looked into cantorial schools when we were dating, but all were in New York and required a year in Israel. I wasn't too fond of the idea. I didn't like New York (especially the Yankees) and my job and family were centered in Massachusetts. I was looking at the *Jewish Advocate* one day and saw a job that I thought would be perfect for Steve. It was in Marblehead, Massachusetts at the Jewish Community Center as the head of youth programming. It got him out of New York and into Massachusetts. It was a good job in theory, but not a great match for Steve.

After leaving the JCC, he needed a job and was having a hard time finding something else in the Jewish community; they all required an advanced degree. My Dad talked to him about working for him in his store. Dad thought it would be a good way for him to get business experience. After a few months, he found a job at the Chestnut Hill Mall selling boots for Timberland.

Over the years, he went from selling boots at Timberland and shoes at Bostonian to jewelry at Kay's. Steve did well in sales, but his heart wasn't in it. After attending a Jewish conference, he decided that he wanted to work in the Jewish community. He was working at Kay Jewelers at the time, and he came back to the store wearing his kippah (head covering) by accident. Someone said "Happy Hanukah." At that point he realized how tired he was working in the secular world.

This time, instead of applying to cantorial school in New York, there was another option. Hebrew College in Newton had a part-time cantorial school that he could go to while working. It meant that he could still be employed and not have to move out of town. He was finally able to fulfill his dream about singing in the Jewish community. He got a part-time job teaching at the local temple while going to school. What he learned was that he loved teaching. He decided to change his course of action; he would be a Jewish Educator but continue in music by writing contemporary Jewish music. He felt that the cantorial school was too rigid. What he really loved was to use his creativity to write.

Over the years, he was starting to find his passion. He wrote music, worked with youth group kids, and taught religious school for all ages. It was hard on him physically. There was a lot of driving and no set schedule. He ate on the road and slept very few hours. During the summer he started to look into working at summer camps. For two summers he worked in Georgia. It was hard for him physically because of the heat and humidity; but he loved living and breathing Jewish music.

On July 4, 2004, I got a call that he was in the hospital because his blood pressure was sky rocketing. When he came home, they did tests and told him he had type two diabetes.

I wasn't surprised, knowing how he conducted his life, but I was surprised by how he dealt with it. We went to the dietician the doctor recommended and, after he went on the diet for a week or two, he was back to his old ways. He always said not to worry -- his numbers were fine.

One summer we worked together at a camp in western Massachusetts. It was a really hard summer for me because I saw how poorly he ate and how difficult it was for him to move around the camp. His legs were always swollen and he had a tough time making it up the hill. I vowed I would never work at a camp again. I felt too old and too aggravated. Steve decided to work again at another camp but my camp days were over!

When I was dealing with my parents and mainly my Dad, I spent less and less time with Steve. We both had crazy schedules and had very little time together. There were many times I went to work or to family functions alone because Steve had a youth group event or concert to attend.

In March 2009, I went to an event alone at Synagogue Council. I bumped into Steve's primary care physician. I remember talking with him and saying I would like to go to the doctor's appointment with Steve. He said it was up to Steve. I told him I was very concerned that Steve was neglecting his health; he wasn't sticking to his diet and wasn't testing himself regularly for diabetes. Again he said it was up to Steve. He said," You and I can't do anything. It is his life."

CHAPTER 4
Meeting with the Rabbi

IN LATE MARCH 2009, I was working at Northeastern Hillel and Rabbi David Winner (who worked with my students) came into my office. He wasn't paid from our organization, but he taught classes and had worked with individual students over the years. The Rabbi was Orthodox and I was Reform, but we had a good relationship.

I talked with him that day because I was very depressed. Work was not going well. The building was having issues. I was overwhelmed with the upcoming Passover holiday, but personally I was frustrated as well. I was forty-four years old and felt stuck. I had been in my job for twelve and a half years and was tired. I wanted to have children but felt that the door was closed. Steve and I both had extremely busy lives and children weren't going to fit into the equation. I don't know why I opened up to him. I thought he would say "It is never too late; it is a mitzvah (good deed) to have children."

He surprised me. He took a totally different approach. He said it was "Beshert" (meant to be) what Steve and I do. "Steve was teaching children from kindergarten to high school affecting hundreds of kids, and you have worked with hundreds of college students over your twelve years in this job. So you could have a kid, but you both have affected hundreds of children."

He said "I want you to get up every day and say the Modeh Ani prayer, thanking God for being alive. After that, write down ten things you are grateful for."

That Rabbi made the biggest impact on me and really gave me the strength to deal with what was coming next.

CHAPTER 5

The Day My World Changed

ON APRIL 7TH I WOKE up early thinking that I could get to work to have a maintenance person fix a leak at the building. I ran downstairs to say good-bye to Steve, but he wasn't in his usual places -- either on the sofa watching TV or at the computer in the dining room. I called out to him, but he wasn't there. I saw the bathroom door was open; he was sitting on the toilet. I said to myself, "That's a new one—he fell asleep on the toilet." I called out, "Steve, wake up!", but got no response. I tried shaking him -- but nothing. Then I panicked. I called 911 and they asked me to see if he had a pulse. Nothing. They said they would be there in a couple of minutes. I paced back and forth. I tried to shake him -- his hands looked discolored - his lips looked blue. I kept saying, "This can't be happening."

After what seemed like an hour the ambulance finally arrived. The EMT came in and went straight to the bathroom. They checked his pulse and said to me, "I'm sorry but he has passed." I was in total shock. I couldn't believe it. I thought they could do *something*.

They had me sit down and try to breathe. I couldn't believe it. I was to-tally in shock. I knew that I had to call his parents. It would be the hardest call I had ever had to make. I dialed the number; his Dad answered. I said, "Steve had a massive heart attack this morning and passed away." Philip couldn't believe it; I heard him yell to Barbara to get out of the shower. I heard her say, "I'm in the shower. Why are you yelling at me?" Then I heard him tell her and heard her wailing in the background; a sound I never wanted to hear again.

How could I tell them that their first born son had just passed away? It was so difficult. I asked them to come to our house right away.

Then I called my sister. I knew she would be at home-- and that I couldn't stay alone. Debra had lost her job the day before, so she wouldn't be at work. I knew this wasn't the time to tell her, but I had to. I then tried to call Temple Emanuel. I got so many messages; I couldn't get through to a person. I was freaking out. Finally I reached our interim rabbi, Rabbi Begosian. She was totally shocked. She told me that Rabbi Ross, the assistant rabbi, would come over because he was in Worcester. She would tell everyone in the temple and then would come back to Worcester to meet with me at the funeral home.

I then called Rabbi Larry Milder, the rabbi at the Westborough temple. I knew he was in town and that Steve had been working there. He and Rabbi Ross both arrived in a few minutes. I was very glad to have them both with me.

They asked me when I wanted to have the funeral. I had no idea; I couldn't even believe it was happening. How could I deal with this type of thing? Debra kept on saying I should do it Friday because it would give me more time. I knew according to Jewish tradition that Friday wouldn't work because it would be during Passover. I talked with Philip and Barbara and decided I would just meet them at the funeral home and make the decision.

I then called Temple Sinai in Sharon and told them. I called Eric Komar (Steve's close friend) who was in shock. I asked him to play *Shalom Rav* (one of Steve's songs) if he could. I called Jordan Millstein (the former Rabbi of Temple Emanuel) and he said he would try to be there -- he did say that he would do a eulogy but not run the service.

I called work and spoke with my boss Sam, Shelli in the Spiritual Life office, and my students. They repeatedly told me not to worry; they would take care of everything.

I called my friends Adam and Lynne Winter and asked them to come over; they took phone calls while we were away.

Debra and I went to the funeral home; Philip and Barbara were already there. We gave the funeral home the pictures and wording to put in the *Boston Globe.* I just couldn't believe that we were doing this. We went to the cemetery and picked out a plot. They asked me if I wanted to get one for myself as well. How would I know- I was only 44 years old!! Would I be alone the rest of my life? I told them to wait.

At last we drove home. I called Roche Brothers to set up the meal for after the funeral. The funeral was going to be the next day at noon. I was worried that people wouldn't know the details for the funeral. Steve's Dad told me don't worry, people will find out.

We later went out to eat with Jeff and Faith (Steve's brother and sister-in-law). Faith came over to the house and helped clean everything out. Within an hour she had decluttered everything. It was amazing!

When she left, it was so quiet in the house. I don't think I had even thought about it before; I was alone. It had all happened in just one day. I was totally exhausted but couldn't think of sleeping. I looked on Facebook and email and saw tons of messages -- not only on my site, but on Steve's as well.

Facebook helped me make it through that night. I couldn't sleep, but everyone's notes and prayers helped me get through.

THE DAY OF THE FUNERAL – APRIL 8, 2009

That morning I got up early and dressed. I listened to a CD of Steve's music, it was strange, but it made me feel better. Philip and Barbara came in when they heard the song *Make it a Bridge.* Philip had never heard it before and was totally blown away.

Philip kept saying, "I need the music to that. I want my cantor to sing it at temple." I was surprised that he had never heard it but more shocked that he thought I would know right where the music was or that I could even think about it right then.

Finally the hearse came and drove us to the temple. It was so strange. I knew that I had gone through this for my mother just a couple of years ago, but I had both of my sisters with me then. This was my husband. I still couldn't believe that he wasn't here anymore.

We all went into the library at the temple and waited for people to come. All of my family came in, and Dad came in with his wheelchair. He looked so weak and in disbelief. I think everyone was still just in total shock.

Not only did Steve's aunt and cousin come in from Florida, but his cousins from Maryland came as well. There were so many people, I just couldn't believe it. When we went into the sanctuary – it was packed! Totally full – like the High Holidays. I guess I didn't have to worry about people finding out about the funeral.

Rabbi Bogosian was leading the service; it was nice but additional people made it extra special. Rabbi Jordan Millstein did an incredible eulogy. Our former cantors Sally Neff and Dan Mutlu sang beautiful melodies from the liturgy of the service. It was so incredible. Eric Komar sang Steve's *Shalom Rav* on Steve's blue guitar. Eric was so shaken up that it took him three times through the introduction to get the courage to sing.

Jeff also gave one of the eulogies. He was very good; he talked about Steve's collections. It was funny but very true. As Molly (Steve's student president) was speaking, I looked around and saw all the kids. It was incredible.

While Jordan was speaking, Rabbi Winner handed me a package. That seemed strange, but I was very glad to see him and have his support. He had been so supportive over the past month, and I was thankful that he had been able to come.

The service was a blur, I don't think I cried because I was still in so much shock.

When they wheeled out the coffin, I was dumbfounded. I couldn't believe Steve was in there. It wasn't real.

I walked toward the hearse with the family and watched the hundreds of people exit the sanctuary. I was totally stunned. I looked at the package that Rabbi Winner had given to me; it was a book called *The Guide to Jewish Mourning*. It was a traditional book, but very helpful.

The cemetery was tough. They conducted a short service, but then they had everyone shovel the dirt on the coffin. Jeff wanted to completely cover the area. Everyone was there for what seemed like an eternity. Philip wanted to take a second turn, but Barbara said, "Don't do it; at least I work out." It was funny, but I think she was just really nervous. Then I took over and said, "Steve you always made me shovel. Even when I broke my wrist." Right then it started to snow. It lasted for just a few seconds, but it seemed as if Steve was laughing down at me.

We finally drove back to the house; people were already eating. All I knew was that we had to get everyone out and have a Passover Seder that evening.

Passover Seders

I used to love Passover. I loved being with family and all the food and music. Steve and I would always bring our guitars and lead singing. My favorite time was when I was with his family and we both sang *Arise My Love* as a love song.

It was sweet, but I also loved when Steve did silly songs like *The Frog Song* or *Pharoah Pharoah*.

Over the past several years, I had led Passover Seders at Hillel. Instead of leading the Reform service with Steve at Hillel, I spent the evening with Steve's family at the Marriott. There was a huge space empty at the table-- not for Elijah, but for Steve. Passover will never be the same. It will always be his Yartzeit (the anniversary of his death) from now on.

I was glad to do the Seder with them, but it was just too strange. Faith was amazing; she made three kitchens at the hotel kosher for Passover, warmed up all the food from home, and then made more. It was incredible. We did the Seder but a more traditional version than I was used to. When a sentence ended with the word "men", Barbara or I would add "and women." Jillian (our niece) and Philip kept having political discussions, and I changed the subject.

I asked everyone to share their favorite Steve story about Passover. It was touching.

CHAPTER 6

I'm Going to Finish
His Work

THAT NIGHT STEVE'S COUSIN JESSICA invited me to stay at the hotel with them. I agreed because the dog was at "camp", and I just didn't want to go home to an empty house. It was starting to really hit me.

Jess and I talked until 2am. I couldn't sleep; I was still so much in a state of shock. I had this thought – "I want to finish Steve's CD." I sat up in bed, took out a pad of paper, and wrote down all of his songs.

Steve had seven songs that were previously recorded -- not enough for a full CD. My thought was to complete that CD. His first big song was *Lo Alecha*. The theme of that song is "It is not your obligation to finish the work but you should not desist from it." **My obligation** was to finish his work; I was going to complete his CD.

My idea was to invite seven people to donate songs to his CD in his memory; I knew which musicians and songs I wanted. It was so clear to me that this was what I wanted to do.

CD PROJECT - 2009

Steve had always wanted to do a CD. His dream was to have a full CD with his original songs. He was so talented, but he never had the chance to get the full CD together.

Over the years, I was like his agent. I would always promote his stuff, but he was too modest. In October 2008 he went to Arizona to record a few of his songs with Scott Leader. His dream was to get one of those songs on the *RUACH CD*. (A song competition through the Reform movement.) His songs were just as good if not better than others, but he wasn't as well known or connected. I felt so bad when he found out that he wasn't going to be on the CD,

So when Steve died, I made it my mission to get a CD done.

His songs were:

Lo Alecha
Lecha Dodi
Shalom Rav
Hinei Matov
Make it a Bridge
V'shamru
Ma Tovu

Three of them were produced for a sampler CD; most people had never heard the others.

On Friday, after Steve passed away, I called Jeff Klepper. Jeff was a cantor who worked with Steve at Temple Sinai in Sharon; I told him about the project. He quickly agreed and said that we could use his song "*La'asok B'divrei Torah*". Steve taught that song to his religious school classes because it figuratively means "to soak up the knowledge of Torah." Steve used it in his classes with *Sponge Bob*, soaking up Torah.

I then called Dan Nichols. He agreed to let us use his song *Chazak* (strength)

On Saturday night I talked with Scott Leader and told him about the project. He loved the idea and had been thinking about doing something like that as well.

It was starting to gel. He told me I should email the artists, and he would get the permission for me.

The other artists were:

Beth Schafer
Josh Nelson
Eric Komar
Rabbi Joe Black
Craig Taubman

Steve Brodsky from Sababa and Union for Reform Judaism (URJ) agreed to produce the CD.   I would give him pictures and info for the liner notes.

First Shabbat without Steve

On Friday, April 10th, there were people at the house all day. It was very drain-ing. I wanted to have Shabbat dinner at my house; I was tired of having meals at a hotel. I wanted to have everyone here. When Janet Milder (the Rabbi's wife from the Westborough temple) came over, I asked her if she could make a kosher dinner for us. Jeff and Faith are both kosher, and I wanted to have a nice meal with them. Janet and Amy Sue (a member of the congregation) made an incredible meal, and my friends Adam & Lynne joined us as well. Their entire family were amazing.

Phillip, Barbara, and I went over to the temple together; Adam and Lynne went on their own. For some reason, traffic on Route 9 was jammed, so we were late. Steve was supposed to lead this Shabbat service. Debbie Morin (teacher at Temple Emanuel) agreed to do it at the last minute. She had a nice voice, but she wasn't a songleader or cantor. They decided to do some of Steve's songs to honor him. Since we came late, we missed Steve's version of the song *Lecha Dodi*.

It was very difficult to hear the congregation singing Steve's *Shalom Rav*. Not because it was his song, but because it sounded so strange to hear it on the keyboard and not a guitar. I said to Barbara "Sing Loud." I was thinking to myself, "Steve must be literally rolling over in his grave." What a horrible thought to come to my mind. I guess it was good to be able to laugh.

After the service, I went up to the rabbi and said that I would like to lead any of the services that summer that Steve was scheduled to do. I don't know how I had the courage to do that, but I really wanted to do it to honor Steve.

When I heard my mother-in law singing, I realized that I had to go to Hava Nashira with her that June. It was a Jewish music conference in Wisconsin. She loved to sing and it would be an honor to spend time with her.

After services I asked her if she wanted to go to the conference. She was surprised and really touched. She said, "You want to go to Hava Nashira with your mother-in-law?" I definitely did-- and she was thrilled to be asked and excited to go back to camp!

I knew that Shabbat wouldn't be the same at Temple Emanuel ever again. Steve had a huge presence there -- not only leading some services, but leading the T'fillah Band and running youth group as well.

I realized then that Steve's passing wasn't just my own private loss, but a public one as well. That is why I decided that I needed to start a blog -- because **everyone** lost Mr. Steve.

CHAPTER 7

Sababa

Sababa Concert, April, 2009

On Saturday night *SABABA* (a Jewish music group) was scheduled to play in Worcester. Steve had been working with people from Temple Sinai for months to promote that concert. It was supposed to be a fundraiser for the youth group to solidify the merger of the two temples into one youth group WESTY.

Steve had worked on all the publicity for months. When Steve died, someone from the band called to see if I would still want to have the concert.

If I were Conservative or Orthodox, there would be no question - it would be canceled. However, as a Reform Jew, I thought the concert had to go on in memory and honor of Steve. He loved music, and this was the best way to honor him.

The youth group and their cantor worked hard on all the last minute arrangements. We didn't know how many people would attend because it was Passover weekend. It could be extremely full to honor his memory or not too busy because many people would be out of town with family.

One thing I was concerned about was Steve's brother. Jeff was much more traditional, and he wouldn't feel comfortable going to a concert. However, no one in the family said anything; they left it up to him to decide.

Since I am so reserved (HUH), I talked with Jeff. "I know that it isn't something that you believe in, but it would mean so much to me and to Steve for you to be at the concert. Music was Steve's life, and it would be amazing if you all could be there."

Jeff and the rest of the family went to the concert. I'm sure it was tough for them but Jeff came up to me after and thanked me for asking him to go.

It was significant that it was **Sababa.** Steve had become very close with the group over the years. He had just recorded music with Scott Leader a few months before, and was close with Steve Brodsky and Robbie Sherwin from CAJE (a Jewish Educator conference) and other Jewish venues.

The youth group was amazing. They put together a slide show that had pictures of Steve with the kids. It was incredible. All the youth group came; they sold tee shirts, and I sold some of Steve's sampler CDs. They led Havdalah (the ceremony to end the Sabbath) and helped out the entire night.

The concert was fantastic. There were about 200-250 people in attendance.   The most powerful part was the end: **Sababa** asked the local Jewish musicians to get on stage to help sing some of Steve's songs. Peter and Ellen Allard, Jeff Klepper, and Larry Milder joined them.

When Scott introduced *Make it a Bridge,* he said "Steve recorded this song in October in Arizona." It was surprising to his family because they didn't know he had gone out there.

I just couldn't leave that as the introduction. Since I was in the front row, I got Steve Brodsky's attention and asked if I could talk about the song.

Make it a Bridge has a lot of significance. It was written in memory of Lenny Zakim of the Anti-Defamation League. The poem was written after the Zakim bridge was dedicated 10 years ago. Steve was so moved by the poem that he wrote music to it. I dedicated the song to Lenny's daughter Shari. She was one of my Hillel students and was in the audience along with about 10 other Hillel students.

It was very moving; I knew then that the CD I wanted to put together should be called ***Make it a Bridge*** instead of ***Lo Alecha.***

CHAPTER 8
Shiva

RIP STEVE MELTZER

A few days after Steve died, Ethan Winter called me and said he wanted to start a group on Facebook in memory of Steve. I thought it was a great idea, but I didn't realize the magnitude of this venture.

Ethan, Meaghan (his sister) and I would be the administrators of the group. I thought it would be a great way for people to post a few comments.

Thanks to the site, I was able to let everyone know when I wanted to do shiva (ritual mourning period) at my house.

Within days there were 700 members. People from all over the world started posting things. People wrote about how they knew Steve - how he influenced their lives. It was truly amazing. After a while I started looking at it often for comfort, and I was dumbfounded to learn how much of an impact he had had on kids of all ages.

Some kids said they took up guitar because of Steve. Others mentioned how they used to hate Hebrew school, but they couldn't wait to be in Mr. Steve's class.

The site has been an incredible comfort for me. Now I look at pictures (sometimes videos) and sometimes smile with tears streaming down my face.

Shiva at home and at work

On Sunday, around the world they were celebrating Easter. I wanted to spend the day with family and friends. I wanted to be able to see my Dad, but I knew that he wouldn't be able to get up the stairs at my house. Our compromise was to meet at a restaurant and the only place that would be good that wouldn't be serving for Easter was Chinese. There goes keeping Passover. I didn't have bread but rice? Oh well.

I was glad to be able to be with my family; I had spent a lot of time with Steve's family, but not mine.

Earlier that weekend I made the decision to have people for Shiva at the house between 4 -7pm. I got home around 1pm and decided to go to Stop & Shop to buy some extra Passover supplies. While I was there, I saw a few people from Congregation B'nai Shalom. We could have had a minyan! (ten people). I saw Steve's doctor; it was very hard to see him-- especially since Steve had an appointment to see him on that Tuesday when he passed away. I just didn't know what to say to him.

I was home for a little while; people started coming at 2pm. "There goes the prospect of having time to myself," I thought. I had a constant flow of people all day, neighbors, friends, kids and adults -- probably about 60 in all. Around 4pm I had my friend Alissa lead a service. When we finished the service, I had everyone explain how they knew Steve and share a story about him. It was really touching. One of the neighbor's kids had Steve as a teacher as well as a music teacher at Camp Tel Noar. She was so broken up - I couldn't believe it. I was very moved by my friend Adina's sharing. She said that she remembered our Uff Ruf (service) before our wedding, and she said that she knew we had found our B'shert (our soulmate) when we sang to each other. I thought that was so nice.

People were at the house for hours. I went into the dining room and saw I had a phone message from Cindy from my temple. She said that I should listen to the Worcester radio station that played Jewish music every Sunday evening; that night they were dedicating the show to Steve. I missed most of it, but I did hear some of it with Margot (another temple member); I was so glad Cindy had called.

On Sunday I emailed my students at Northeastern Hillel and said I would come in and do a Shiva there as well on Monday night. They sent out an email and we had dinner (there was so much extra food from the Seders). Surprisingly, about 35 people came-- some alumni and students. It was great to see some of the people who graduated that I hadn't seen in a while.

I had invited a Rabbi from Hebrew College to help. She was late so Molly Simpson (one of the alumni) led it, which made the service very special. I realized that a lot of the freshmen never met Steve. The older students knew him well from Reform services, dinners or high holidays.

My favorite shares were all the references to Steve's great guitar playing for Reform services. Many mentioned his great brisket recipe for Passover. The best memory was from Gordon Dale (a former student); he told the story about Steve's adventure with David Broza (a famous Israeli musician)

Gordon recalled that Steve had approached him (Gordon is really into Jewish music as well) and said,"You would never believe who I spent Sunday night with --David Broza." He was doing a concert in Worcester and Steve was on the planning committee, so after the concert he went out with about 5 others from the committee for Sushi with David Broza.

When the chef came up to the table, he asked what everyone wanted to eat David Broza said, "You are the artist, you create," so the chef made the best sushi ever. After dinner Broza told the chef and the rest of the group, "You shared your art, now I will share mine." He took out his guitar and played for an hour in the restaurant.

Steve was like a little kid. He was so excited; he showed his passion and his excitement in everything he did.

What I learned from this experience is if you ever have to lead a Shiva (or memorial service), don't just do the service. Have everyone share something about the person. You will learn amazing stories that you may never have known about that person. It also brings the group much closer together.

CHAPTER 9

Public Mourning
& Blog Posts

MANY OF THE EXCERPTS FROM this part of the book are from my blog. I thought it was more authentic about what was happening at the time of Steve's passing.

INTRO TO PUBLIC MOURNING

I decided to write a blog rather than just do a regular journal because I feel that social networking is a huge phenomenon. When I lost my husband last April, one of the things that kept me going was all the outpouring of Facebook messages from friends and family around the world. In other generations, when someone died you had to call dozens of people to get the word out. When Steve died, I called about ten people and there were 600 people at the funeral. People are very connected through social networks, Facebook groups, email lists etc. Over the year I would post something about Steve and I would get dozens of responses. People don't get on the phone or visit anymore -- they check blogs, twitter and Facebook.

I also wanted to create this as a resource for others who may be going through a sense of loss themselves. I am not an expert, but I feel that writing about my experiences may be helpful for others as well.

I thought a blog would be better than writing a book because I don't have the time or expertise to write an entire book, but this is more stream of consciousness. Hopefully, it will be helpful not only for me but also for others in their healing process.

SCHMUTZIE

At 35 Steve got it in his head that he wanted a dog. He never had one as a child, and he thought that it would be great to have one.

At the time Steve was working at a mall, and one of the vendors who had a cart near his store had a dog who was about to give birth to puppies. One day Steve came home all excited and said "The dog had 12 puppies! I am going to drive down to Rhode Island to pick one up."

That is how we got Schmutz. Steve saw that she was the only one with a brownish color and he loved the look. I remember him bringing her home, she was so tiny and adorable!

That was 11 years ago.

When Steve died, Schmutzie was very affected by it. I don't know if she saw him that morning, but she knew something was wrong. After my sister came over on April 7th, I asked my neighbor to take Schmutzie to camp (Pedigree Playland) I knew it would be too hard to deal with walking the dog with all that was going on.

A week later, I brought Schmutzie home. She looked around the family room; she knew something wasn't right. She didn't want to go in. Finally she did but was very clingy. The next morning I saw that she had been sick; I went to the vet who said dogs are very affected by losses. So strange how dogs sense that something is wrong.

Schmutzie has been my best friend over the past 9 months. I hate taking her out in the snow and cold, but she is still there to give me a kiss or hug if I need it.

HOW ARE YOU?

How are you? It is one of the hardest questions I'm asked. I can always tell if someone has no idea about Steve; they say it with a sweet tone not really wanting to know but say it out of routine.

If a friend says *"How are you?"* they say it with a different tone. They also tilt their head and have a concerned look on their face.

Those are the hard times. How am I? What am I supposed to say? Do I just say fine? Should I be truthful? Do they even really want to know?

So the answer is "it depends." Some days are much better than others. I started this blog because this is a way I can write how I am without saying it aloud.

The first entries were all about the first week. Why do I remember every detail of that week but the rest of the summer is a blur? I remember some events, but I don't remember what I did in between.

At work during the summer, I tried to concentrate, but I couldn't really do it. Instead I tended to look at email and Facebook because everything else took too much concentration.

Once my students came back in September, I felt much more back to "Normal" because I was much busier and didn't "stay in my head" the entire time.

STEVE'S CAR

If you knew Steve, then you know his car. It doesn't mean that you have driven in it. WHY? Because it could be hazardous to your health. Steve's entire life was in the car. The front seat was always so cluttered with stuff that one time Steve picked me up from something and told me to sit in the back seat because there was no way that I could fit in the front.

Anyway, when Laurie Porter (from my temple) offered to help clean the car with me, I jumped at the chance. I did however "pre-clean" before she got to the house. When I saw the front seat, I was blown away. There was so much junk that I couldn't believe it. I cleaned out so many fast food wrappers, seltzer bottles, soda cans; it was gross. I also made a lot of money! I found uncashed checks, cash, and gift cards. It was unbelievable.

When Laurie got to the house, I had the front seat all done. It still took a long time to clean out the rest of the car. There were tons of boxes, books, files and backpacks. I felt that it was such a great accomplishment when it was completely empty. (after about 2 hours). I gave Laurie a few boxes for the temple. I put a lot of stuff in the garage and in the "music" room.

Adam offered to put the car on Craig's List. Beforehand, he offered to take it in to be fixed and detailed. When it came back, it looked like a brand new car. After a couple of months, Adam told me that he was going to buy it for his son Ethan. I was psyched that they were getting it. I decided that if I sold the car, I would go on a trip. Italy--here I come!

CHAPTER 10

Hava Nashira

Steve and his Mom (Other Mom) at Jillian Meltzer's Bat Mitzvah

EACH YEAR STEVE AND I went to Oconomowoc, Wisconsin for Hava Nashira, a Jewish music conference. It was our favorite time of the year. It is a time that we sing with the most amazing people from all over the United States and beyond.

When Steve died, we had already paid for the registration. I was wondering how I could go without him. It was our favorite week together. So when I sat next to Steve's Mom at services, I just knew that we should go together (see the first Shabbat)

I decided that I would fly with her from New York and spend time with Steve's cousins in Maryland before the trip. I was excited about Hava Nashira (HN) but also kind of scared. This was the first time I would see a lot of our really close friends. Although it would be hard for both of us, it would be very moving.

I think the most amazing part was talking with the artists individually, they were so down to earth and I felt very close to them. All our friends were supportive and loving.

One of the most moving parts was when Josh Nelson played Steve's *Shalom Rav* in the service and then Peter and Ellen played it during Shabbat.

I decided to introduce the idea of the CD to everyone. I would not only introduce it, but also sing Steve's *Make it a Bridge*. I knew it would be too hard for me to sing alone, so I asked my friend David to come up with me. We actually had Steve's song piped into the PA system and sang with him on the chorus. It was remarkable.

It was not only an incredible week of music, but it brought my mother-in law and me closer than ever. We shared a very strong bond; we had both lost a huge part of our lives. We were able to laugh, sing and cry together. I knew that it was a very special HN. Steve's spirit was definitely there.

CHAPTER 11

Biking in Tuscany

Sienna, Italy
July 2009

WHEN I SOLD MY CAR, I decided that some of the money would go to the trip I had always dreamed of taking --- a bike trip in Italy. I knew it was a trip that I could never do with Steve, because it was pretty rigorous, and he would be at camp most summers. It was always just a pipe dream. Since I knew that I could no longer make excuses about money or Steve not being able to go along, I decided to go.

After college I had biked through the Loire Valley in France, and it was an incredible trip. I thought it would be great to do it in Italy. I decided on Tuscany. I loved the idea of seeing Italy by bike. I signed up through Vermont Bike Tours and went in July.

I posted that I was planning to go and couldn't believe how many responses I got. Take me with you... make sure to see xyz or ... go to this restaurant... All I knew was I was getting to do something I loved to do: bike, drink good wine, and eat!

My trip was amazing. The people were incredibly friendly, and the biking though difficult, was spectacular. I challenged myself physically as well as mentally. I was able to be alone if I wanted or to spend time with groups as well.

I loved Florence. It was so romantic and beautiful. I kept on thinking Steve would have loved it.

One of my favorite stories from Italy is from when we were in Florence. I was walking with two of my friends when we bumped into an Italian shopkeeper. He showed us his store. He was a designer who owned a leather store. He showed me this amazing red leather reversible coat. "It was like butta" (the joke from **Saturday Night Live** making fun of Barbra Streisand saying butta not butter) He said something like "It is better than the *schmutas* you get in United States" I asked him "Did you just say something in Yiddish?" He said yes. I asked if he was Jewish and he said yes and I said I was as well. He said

"Mishpacha" (family). He took out his calculator and said "because you are *mishpacha* instead of $1500 Euros I will charge you $1,000" I just started laughing. I told him I loved the coat, but I couldn't buy it. I asked if I could take a picture with him in the coat and he agreed. That is my story about my Italian friend Philipo

CHAPTER 12
The First Year and Beyond

HIGH HOLIDAYS

One of the hardest things to deal with is the holidays. In early May I had
to interview potential Rabbis for Hillel High Holiday (Rosh Hashanah and
Yom Kippur) services. Normally, I lead the Reform services with the students and hire someone for the Conservative. Sometimes Steve helped. The
past year he did the Torah reading, did a sermon in song and used one of
Rabbi Joe Black's songs.

This year I called Hebrew College and the Rabbi in charge of placement
said "It's awfully late to start looking. Usually people call around Passover or
before." I said to him that I really couldn't do it then. I didn't want to get into
why but then I realized that this rabbi actually knew Steve. He used to work
with him in Canton. Either he just was insensitive or he didn't realize that I
was Steve's wife. I said that I had just lost my husband, so I really didn't have
the opportunity to do anything until then. I could hear him gulp. I realized
right then that he didn't realize I was Steve's widow. He felt horrible. I asked
if there was any way to post the job; I would greatly appreciate it.

Within a day I had several excellent resumes. I started to interview can-
didates. It was extremely difficult to stay focused. I knew that "my Ideal
candidate" would be able to lead a combined service so I wouldn't have to lead
the Reform service myself.

I asked them about themes for sermons and their experience leading High Holiday services. I think the hardest thing was when someone talked about the liturgy for Yom Kippur *"Who should live and who should die."* I totally lost it; I apologized and actually told the candidate that it was very hard to do these interviews because I had just lost my husband at Passover.

I finally selected someone, but it was difficult. I didn't have the ability to concentrate; I wasn't following up as well as I should. I really doubted if I could pay attention to the details to help with High Holidays.

During the holiday, I wanted to say to the Rabbi, "I need you to take care of everything. I need to be able to just be a congregant." That wasn't happening. However, I was able to sit through services this year. It was hard not being with any of my family. Luckily my students have been like a family for so long.

I made it through, but I missed being with Steve - hearing him blow the shofar or play the guitar for the service

MEETING WITH THE REGIONAL DIRECTOR OF HILLEL

During the summer after Steve died, I met with the Regional Director of Hillel, whom I have known since I was in college. I always liked working with him because he helped not only to get me my job at Northeastern but at MIT Hillel as well. That day we met and he talked about my future at Northeastern. Sam had lost his wife 10 before, so he knew what I was going through, trying to keep it together personally and professionally.

Since it was summer, it was quiet at work. He said that he thought it would be a good idea if I stayed for one more academic year. He knew that my heart wasn't in it anymore – not the way it had been before Steve died. I should work the next academic year, but my main focus would be to find a new job that would be less stressful for me.

I was hurt, but I knew he was right. I loved a lot of aspects of my job at Northeastern, but other parts were draining me. The problem was I had no idea what I would do.

I spent the rest of the year at Hillel, going on some interviews, but not having any luck. The funny thing was the board decided to lighten my load of the fundraising obligations that year, so I spent most of the time on the programmatic "stuff", and I really enjoyed it. I knew that it was time to leave. I just didn't know what I could find.

UNVEILING

Unveiling, November 2010, B'nai B'rith Cemetery, Worcester, MA

We all decided that we would do the unveiling in November before Barbara and Philip went to Florida. Barbara and I worked together to design the gravestone. We both knew it had to be like Steve.

We also decided to keep the ceremony to just family. I knew that it was hard enough as it was and I didn't want to worry about whom to invite. We decided to have a kosher meal after the service at the temple since Steve's brother's family were all kosher.

Rabbi Berger did the ceremony. As I thought about it, I realized that Steve never really got to know our new rabbi. He met him for a couple of minutes when the rabbi was interviewing, but he didn't officially start until after Steve died.

The rabbi did a very nice job. At the end, I started Julie Silver's song *Shir Chadash,* because on the gravestone we engraved two guitars and the words "*Sing unto God a New Song*". I think Steve would have approved of our selection.

After the weekend, I posted the picture on Facebook and got so many comments from people. I think people felt they were with us by sharing the picture.

BIENNIAL

Union of Reform Judaism Convention, Toronto 2009

On November 4-8th, I went to Biennial in Toronto. It is an international conference for Reform Judaism held every other year in different locations throughout the country. I first wanted to go because the CD was supposed to be done, and they were going to sell it during the convention. However, it was running really late and wouldn't be done until after the first of the year (at least)

I was kind of nervous going to Biennial alone. Usually, Steve and I went together but this time I flew alone. Also only one person went from our temple. Usually we have a big group. Before I went, Sue Summit told me to watch out for Zoe (her daughter) since it would be her first time. Zoe got the WESTY scholarship to go to the conference.

I was excited to stay with my long-time friend Leslie Grossman. We hadn't spent too much time together since she moved to North Carolina, so it would be a great time to catch up. Leslie and I had been friends since we were in youth group in high school.

I flew on Porter Airlines, which was a new airline Fare was only $99 and was excellent. It went right to the city, then had a ferry to a bus that went straight to our hotel.

The conference itself was good; I loved all the music and seeing everyone.

The big events were difficult. I would go to the session and look around and not see anyone I knew. Usually I would have gone in with Steve. Leslie was at her booth, so I would just look around. It was frightening.

One time I looked up; images of camp were on the screen. I thought of Steve and how he would have loved to be at this conference. He lived for them. He didn't care too much about the sessions, but preferred to hang out with his friends, singing and staying up late watching the musical acts.

I looked up at the screen and started to cry. Then I saw Julie Silver; she gave me a huge hug; she invited me to sit with her and gave me a copy of her new CD. She said "I know it is hard, but we are all here for you."

Another hard moment was on Shabbat. I walked over to the room designated for New England participants, and there was a table full of Westborough people and the two people from Worcester. There wasn't any room at the table. I felt like I was back in junior high. Right then I heard a small voice say "sit with us." Zoe Summit asked me to sit with her and her friends. It was the nicest gesture yet!

The rest of the conference was very nice; I loved all the music and on the last day, I had a long walk from the hotel to the airport. It was about 70 degrees out, and I kept on walking enjoying the beautiful weather.

VALENTINE'S DAY

Steve was a huge romantic. Even though Valentine's Day is not a Jewish holiday (Just ask Rabbi Joe Black), Steve and I would always do something special.

One of my favorite memories of Valentine's Day was waking up to a playlist of Love Songs. Steve put together about 23 love songs on a playlist and that was the alarm on the clock. It was truly a gift of love. That evening he made a dinner from scratch, and it was better than any restaurant that we could have gone to.

This year I burned a copy of the CD for Steve's mom for their couples' Valentine's Day party.

Here is a list of love songs - maybe it will be romantic for others on this day.

Valentine's Day Is Not A Jewish Holiday (That's Why I Didn't Buy You Flowers)
Do You Love Me
Love Me Do

My Girl
Puppy Love
It Had To Be You
Maybe I'm Amazed
Have I Told You Lately
Wonderful Tonight
Love Is Here to Stay
Unforgettable
You Send Me
The Way You Look Tonight
Don't Know Why
At Last
More Than Words
My Cherie Amour
Your Body Is A Wonderland
Let's Get It On
Can't Get Enough of Your Love Babe
Could It Be I'm Falling in Love
Shining Star
Breathe
You're Still The One
Unchained Melody
What a Wonderful World
Let's Stay Together
Sexual Healing

Julie Silver posted on Facebook today "What is the most romantic love song?" I have to say *Ani Ohev Otach* (I love you in Hebrew). It is really corny but Steve made a stuffed dog for me. He recorded the song and when you touch the paw it sings.

One day during the summer, I was moving some things in the room and saw the dog; and by accident I touched the paw and heard him sing. It was the hardest thing to hear. I listen to Steve's music all the time, but this was just freaky hearing a dog sing. If Schmutzie started singing to me then, I would have gone to the loony bin!

PASSOVER 2010
This year I went with Barbara and Philip to Jeff and Faith's for the first night of Passover. Faith cooked the meal for Passover. So much food. I knew even last year that I wouldn't want to be at Hillel for the first night. It was important for all of us to be together. It was really good to be with everyone. It felt strange to not have Steve at the table with us. I realized how horrible everyone else sounds without his voice.

We all sang the *Frog Song,* but it was mostly "Other Mom" and myself. We did the entire Seder and finished at midnight. Marc (my nephew) sang the entire ending of the Seder. I was really glad that I was able to share Passover with them.

YARTZEIT
This has been a very difficult week for the Meltzer family. Not only was it Passover and Steve's Birthday, but also the one year anniversary of his passing (Yartzeit).

On Friday night I went down to New York and went to Temple with "Other Mom and Dad" It was really nice seeing them, but very strange to be at their house without Steve. I also stayed in his room and looked at one of our wedding pictures; Steve fixing Jeff's bowtie with me watching in the background.

At services they forgot to put Steve's name in the Yartzeit listing. I think it may have been because the actual Hebrew date is Sunday and it would be considered the next week. However, we wanted to do it that night because I was in from Boston and was there for Passover.

The Cantor played Steve's *Shalom Rav*. It was so strange to hear him sing Steve's song. He also played it very fast-- much different from all the other times I've heard it.

That night I wrote a poem; I couldn't sleep, so at least something good came out of a sleepless night.

HAPPY BIRTHDAY STEVE

Today was a very difficult day. It would have been your 46th birthday. While driving to work, I heard Elton John's *Your Song* and I just lost it. I miss you so much. I know everyone misses you as well. You should see Facebook. Everyone is posting away!

I wrote you a poem.
I hope you like it.......

As the Crocus and the daffodil come sprouting through the earth
I should be celebrating the anniversary of your birth.

Instead I am commemorating the yartzeit of your death
This poem has been written by your loving wife Beth.

Some will remember on the date of April seven
Instead we will do it on the holiday where we don't eat leaven.

Shalom Rav, Lo Alecha and Lecha Dodi
These were your first great songs on your sampler CD

Lo Alecha was your first in your collection.
Nine other artists were asked to contribute a song because of your special Jewish musical connection.

Thank you to Josh, Joe, Jeff, Eric, Beth, Craig, and members of Sababa
And a very special thanks to your ima and your aba

So on April 7th we will reveal "Make it a Bridge"
So put this poem as a reminder on a magnet on the fridge

MAKE IT A BRIDGE

CD arrived April 7, 2010

The CD arrived today at 3pm FedEx --- I was so excited. The CD came out really well. Thanks to Steve Brodsky for all your hard work! I am listening to *Hinei Ma Tov* while typing this. It seems really strange to have the CD done. It was just a dream that finally became a reality.

The pictures look great along with all the other artwork; I am very excited. The neat thing is to hear the other songs I chose to add. I forget that it isn't just Steve's sampler. Then I wonder "Why is that song there? Oh yes, I remember why we chose those songs."

CD IS NOW AVAILABLE!

It has been a few weeks since the CD came out, but today I decided to look at the website and see how it is progressing. It is truly amazing. Everyone has to see the great job Steve Brodsky is doing. He is combining the songs with lyrics and comments from everyone. It is great.

I decided to buy 150 CD's so I can sell them to the temples where Steve worked. I knew it would be hard for everyone to go online; I want it to be easy for people to buy one. If you want one, I will have them at my house or on me at all times

CHAPTER 13

Double Play - Losing Dad

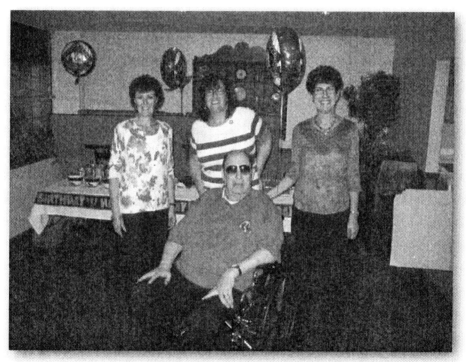

Dad's 80th Birthday, with Debra and Hope,
June 2010

AFTER STEVE DIED, THE ATTENTION shifted to Dad. He had deteriorated a lot since my Mom had died in 2006. He went from living in his home to an assisted living facility. My sisters split responsibilities after the house was sold. I was in charge of "Bills and Pills." I paid all the bills that came to me after they sold the house, and I went over every week to set up the pills. Hope did a lot of the every-day things since she lived close, and Debra took Dad to doctors' appointments.

When there was an emergency, we were all there at the hospital-- at least in shifts. What was most troubling to me was to see Dad lose interest in things. He used to be so social, and many times he didn't want to go to the events at his assisted living facility.

He used a wheelchair now instead of a walker and fought the nurse on hygiene issues. It was sad to see him that way. In January 2011, I was talking with my sister and brother-in-law about replacing his wheelchair because his was somehow broken. We were talking about Dad's lack of desire to be coop-erative, and how he seemed to be giving up.

When my Dad was living at home, before he moved to the assisted living facility, we hired a woman who stayed with him during the day. Dad liked her so we decided that after he moved, she would work a couple of days a week to keep him company, and do some light housework. Another reason we kept her was that she was the eyes and ears for us in terms of his health and wellness. She told us that he had been really negative lately and uncooperative. She said to him, "Fred if you don't take care of yourself, we will have to talk about nurs-ing homes."

I think that set him off. The last place that he wanted to be was in a nursing home. He wanted some independence, and they were a kiss of death in his eyes.

On January 6, 2011, I got a call from my sister Debra that Dad had passed away in the middle of the night. The weird thing was I was feeling that he chose his time. Dad didn't want to suffer or live life that way anymore.

I was very sad, but felt a sense of relief for him. He wasn't suffering. He lived 81 ½ years and his body just gave out.

I made the ride to Andover and Debra and I met with the Rabbi at the Temple. Hope was in California on a business trip, so we had to discuss all the arrangements with her over the phone.

The Rabbi knew my Dad well, so it was easy for him to put together the eulogy. We had the funeral two days later at Temple Emanuel. A lot of people came. It was surreal, three funerals in five years. Dealing with death and funerals wasn't something you wanted to know how to deal with.

My sisters and I talked and I said that I wanted to give one of the eulogies. Hope was away so that would be too difficult and Debra said she would do it but she had written one for our Mom. I was the closest to our Dad and it meant the most to me. Hope's husband Alan also gave one because he was very close to Dad as well.

Here is the eulogy that I gave that day at my Dad's funeral

I am honored to be giving this eulogy on behalf of my "older" sisters Debra and Hope. If you had to describe our Dad in one word it would be mensch. He was a hard-working, fun loving, and caring individual. He would always put everyone else's needs before his own. There were four things that he was very passionate about; his family, his business, his community work and his Boston sports teams.

Dad was a devoted husband, father and grandfather. He loved our mother Adele and was happily married for 51 years. Mom and Dad first lived in a small red house in Lowell on Hovey Street, where they raised their three girls. It was a difficult task for our Dad living with four females and one bathroom! So in 1970 we moved to Andover with a bigger house but,, more importantly 3 bathrooms.

Memories of growing up revolved around family celebrations -- whether it was birthdays, weddings, anniversaries or holidays. Whatever the occasion, there was always chocolate!

Fred and his twin brother Bob worked for the family business Scottie Industries after college at University of South Dakota. They took over the business in the late 1960s when their father Walter passed away. The business was in Lowell, and in the early 1970s, Bob and Fred built a new factory in Hudson, New Hampshire.

Debra, Hope, and I all worked in the factory while growing up -- whether it was pulling rubber off the sneakers or helping out in the store. Through working for our Dad we learned many life lessons about working hard, treating employees fairly, and being an ethical person.

Dad worked hard his whole life -- and most of the time 6 days a week. During the '80s, much of manufacturing went overseas; finally Bob and Fred decided to stop all manufacturing and have just the retail store. In the early '90s, they sold the business. It was very difficult for our Dad to retire; he wasn't the kind of person who would play golf or have a particular hobby. He devoted more time to his other passion: community work.

In Lowell he was on the board of Temple Beth El; when we moved to Andover, he became very involved at Temple

Emanuel. He was on the board, and his proudest memory was choosing our current rabbi during the rabbinic search. Aside from the work at the temple, he was awarded "Man of the Year" for State of Israel Bonds and his involvement in the Merrimack Valley Jewish Federation.

Dad had special memories of his college experience at University of South Dakota. He and Bob couldn't afford schools in the East, so they found USD-- which was only $32 a semester. Dad would always talk about not having money to come home, so he would hitch a ride on the cattle cars.

Dad and Uncle wanted to help other students who couldn't afford an education, so they established the Mascott Foundation at the Beacon School of Management at University of South Dakota. It was so heart-warming to read essays from students who would thank them for giving them the opportunity to get an education.

Our Dad also worked with the Salvation Army. Scottie Industries would donate sneakers to the organization so that people would have shoes for their kids. Every year Mom and Dad would volunteer at Christmas to fit the children in their new sneakers.

In December 2006, our world changed. Our Mom, Adele Feingold Mascott, passed away at the age of 74. Mom was the center of his life and a little spark went out when she passed. A year after she died, we sold the house in Andover-- which was very emotional for Dad. He moved to Marland Place, an assisted living facility in Andover. Over the next four years he slowly got acclimated to the place. He liked joking with the nurses, playing cribbage with some of the guys, or singing along with the musicians who visited weekly.

Throughout those four years, Debra, Hope, and I visited him at least weekly. One of Debra's favorite memories was watching Dad's excitement when he played with the dogs. He loved when Debra brought her dog Chester to Marland Place. But he loved all our dogs (we never had them growing up) Debra first bought Jackson, then Bridgett, and now Chester. I have Schmutzie and Hope has Teddy.

Hope's favorite memories were of the times Dad had spent with his grandchildren Jared and Lindsay. When they were little, Papa and Nanny would help babysit for Hope when she traveled. She also loved discussing business with Dad and really valued his expertise. Sometimes Mom and Dad would come into the office and help out on one of the mailings -- either stuffing or putting labels on envelopes.

My favorite time was watching sports with Dad. We would go to Red Sox games with him when he had season tickets in the late 1970s. We would watch Red Sox and Patriots games "religiously" every week when I visited him at Marland. One Sunday, I came in and Dad looked exhausted. I asked him why he hadn't slept. He said that he had stayed up until 2 am watching the Red Sox vs the Angels. That is dedication!

Over his 80 years, Dad celebrated a lot of milestones. Just this past June we celebrated his 80th birthday at Marland Place, with his favorite make your own sundaes.

Dad was very proud to have three weddings for his girls. He loved his sons in-law like his own: Hope's husband Alan, Debra's husband Steven, and my late husband Steve. He was very excited when Jared and Lindsay were born. He was able to be there for both Jared's Bar Mitzvah and Lindsay's Bat Mitzvah.

And finally, as a sports fan, he was able to see the Red Sox win two World Series, the Patriots win three Super Bowl Championships, and the Celtics and Bruins wave their banners in the Boston Garden.

Whether you call him Fred, "Big Fred", Dad or Papa, we love you and will miss you.

It was hard seeing my Uncle (my Dad's twin) because they looked so much alike. You could tell it was very difficult for him because he had spoken with our Dad every day.

Hope had a Shiva at her house after the service and cemetery, but I wanted to host one as well the next day. I had a lot of close friends and they wanted to come. I hosted between thirty and forty people.

When it was all over, I felt very empty. So much of my life those days had revolved around taking care of my Dad. The day of the funeral I read on Facebook that a famous Jewish songwriter (Debbie Friedman) had died.

During the drive out to Andover, I listened to her music. It was interesting that the two biggest Jewish music influences in my life died within days of each other.

A month after her death, the Boston Jewish community held a memorial concert for Debbie Friedman. It was incredible to see how many people came out to support her music and her influence in Jewish music.

After the concert, I went out with friends. One girlfriend mentioned that she was traveling that summer on a cruise to the British Isles. She wanted to see if anyone would go with her because it was more fun to go with a friend -- and the single supplement was very expensive. I had always wanted to see London and this trip would go to Ireland, Scotland and Wales as well. I said I was interested. She then told me that it was a Jewish singles cruise. I thought why not -- I am single!

CHAPTER 14

Starting a New Chapter

I KNEW THAT IN ORDER to move on in my life I had to de-clutter my house. After Steve died, I got rid of all his clothes and his car right away, but there was so much more "stuff". I always described his passion for electronics and guitars and musical equipment as his "toys" It just took over the house: from the office which had computers and disks everywhere, to the basement with cassettes from Grateful Dead concerts and old files from school, to the music room which housed not only his blue guitar but electric guitar, two acoustic guitars, amps and affect boxes. Everything was overwhelming. Instead of dealing with it, I just left it there.

For a while, I had so much clutter in the bedroom that I couldn't really make the bed. I had paperwork all over the comforter, piles of mail everywhere, and laundry baskets full of Steve's ties and kippot (head coverings).

De-cluttering was really like an onion. I started with one layer but it just kept going deeper and deeper. One thing I realized was that I couldn't do this project alone-- it was just too much. Every time I tried, I got frustrated and moved onto something else. I had the intention, but I just couldn't do it.

One day I asked my friend Peter to come over. He worked for a music store in Worcester. He spent hours with me going through the music room. He took crates of equipment. I ended up selling Steve's three guitars, his amp and a lot of other "stuff" that I just would never need. But I would keep his Blue Guitar -- that was Steve's baby. His Taylor was his pride and joy. Even though I had kept it for a couple of years, I never played it. It was his. The only person who played it in that time was Eric Komar at Steve's funeral.

Steve had a blue mandolin. I had no idea how to play it. I knew it was probably worth something, but why just keep it? I thought of Steve's friends from the band Sababa. Robbie played mandolin. One day while I was looking through the music room, I saw the mandolin and decided to send Robbi a message. "I was thinking of you when I saw Steve's mandolin." She called me on the phone. She was close to Steve because they went to many music and educator conferences together. I knew her, but not well. I asked, "Robbi, would you want the mandolin?" She was shocked. I told her that I would give it to her; she just had to pay for shipping. She was very moved; it really meant a lot to her.

After a couple of months, I got a call from Peter. They had sold the guitars and some of the musical equipment. He asked me if I wanted a check for the items sold or a store credit. Since I didn't need any more "stuff", I decided to get a check. Not knowing how much it was I was surprised when I saw the check was for $350. I didn't just want to deposit the check; I wanted it to mean something because it was Steve's musical equipment. I recently had received a message on Facebook from the members of Sababa that they were creating a new CD. They were doing a "Kickstarter" fundraising project to pay for the CD. It was a pretty new idea. I thought that donating the money from the sale of Steve's musical equipment would be a fitting way to support their new CD. They had a special category for "double chai" $360. (Chai meant life so it was double life) I decided to give that amount. It entitled me to a framed signed CD, 10 copies of their new CD, and one copy of all their previous CDs. It was more important to me that I was honoring Steve's memory by helping his friends.

I received more money from the sales, and a year later I was pleased to help Eric Komar on his new CD as well.

CHAPTER 15

Dating Again

I THINK ONE OF THE hardest things to know is when it is ok to date. I knew that I wouldn't stay a widow for the rest of my life. I was in my 40's and too young to write everything off, but I knew I didn't want to go the online dating route or go to bars.

I heard a commercial for a club called Events and Adventures, that sounded like an interesting idea. It was more of a social club that had a variety of fun events to meet people. I went to a couple of events, but I just wasn't that into the scene. For a while I started seeing people who were mutual friends of Steve and myself. It was hard because there was too much history. I also didn't know how to act in a new relationship. Were people judging me if I started dating? Was it too soon? Was I too picky? Was I comparing too much or expecting too much?

In March 2011, I felt like I was hitting rock bottom. I was miserable at my job. There was a new dean who brought in a consultant to shake things up. He gave everyone a quota. If you didn't reach it you would be fired. In recruiting I had had quotas, but they were more guidelines not ultimatums.

After that day I was a wreck. I had just put money down on a brand new car. I got a great trade-in for my old one because it had very few miles on it. I wanted to trade my old car because it had belonged to my parents and reminded me of them every day I drove it.

Meanwhile, there was the ultimatum. I woke up the next morning – with hives. I had never had that problem before. I was freaking out. It was the first time I had made a huge monetary decision on my own without a husband or my father. Now I had no one to fall back on. I wasn't nervous about losing my job, but the prospect of it petrified me. I would be alone with a new car and no job! I went back to the dealership and told them the story. I couldn't get out of the deal. They gave me a free month without any payments -- not great but at least something.

That month I worked really hard and tried to get the group to work together. The other recruiter and I made quota, but three people were fired. It was so unfair. Those three hadn't been recruiters before that month!

I just knew I needed something else. I decided to enroll in a master's program and start courses that spring. I felt it would help propel my career. I enrolled at Northeastern in a Masters in Leadership with a certificate in Non-Profit Management. Classes were offered both in person and on-line.

I was also working part-time as a youth advisor at Temple Emanuel in Worcester. They had hired a temporary person after Steve died; I decided to apply for the opening that next year. I wanted to do it because I wasn't working within the Jewish community at Northeastern anymore and it would be a good opportunity to work with high school students. It was very satisfying because many of the group had worked with Steve in the past. In some way I saw it as a way to finish his work.

In March I was seeing someone I had known for a long time. We got along well, but it was very difficult to make plans. I remember trying to see if we could do one night of Passover together. He had lost his Dad a year before so he felt a strong obligation to be with his Mom for the holiday and to not invite anyone else. It was becoming very uncomfortable trying to make plans with him.

I decided to go to New Jersey to see my friend Eric at his CD Release party. I remember talking with Eric ahead of time, he said he might play a couple of Steve's songs (kind of a "heads- up") I was bracing myself for it. Eric and Steve were very close friends; Eric had stayed at our house many times when he was recording his first CD. They played at each other's concerts.

Eric's concert was great -- and then it just ended. He never played any of Steve's songs. I was very upset; maybe because it was so emotional to see Eric playing without Steve. But also I was expecting to hear Steve's music. When it didn't happen, I was wasn't angry-- but hurt. I ran out to the bathroom and cried for a while. I just didn't know why I was so emotional; usually I don't get upset in public.

I decided to tell Eric that I was going home right away. It was just too emotional for me. Originally, I was going to stay for dinner with his family, but I wasn't in the mood. I also didn't want to bring down the rest of his family. They were all in such great spirits after the concert.

I drove home upset and lonely. I felt that the last remembrance of Steve was gone. I was stuck in traffic on the George Washington Bridge when Eric called me. He apologized and admitted that he skipped the songs on purpose. The songs he was playing at the concert were all so upbeat, and he didn't want to ruin the flow of the concert. I told him I understood. I was still upset; I guess I was wondering why he couldn't acknowledge his best friend and play one of his songs.

That week was hard. I had no plans for one of the nights of Passover. I broke up with the guy I was seeing, and I was preparing to have fifteen people for Passover on the second night. I didn`t ever cook for a huge crowd so I decided to have it catered. The first night I was all alone, so I practiced for the next night.

Friday night before Passover, I went to Temple in Worcester. I thought I would be commemorating Steve's Yartzeit (the second year anniversary of his death). He died on Passover so I thought that it would be the Friday night before the Seders. I went to services but didn't see his name on the list. They were commemorating it the following week.

I was upset because I had come all the way out there, and I was emotionally ready for the service. While waiting for the service to start, I saw a guy who looked familiar, but I couldn't place him. I asked my friend, but she had no idea either.

At Temple Emanuel, there are only 20 -30 people who attend regularly, so I usually know everyone. After the services, the guy came up to me. He said that we met in October at a Marlborough Chamber of Commerce event. I was there representing Becker College, and he was there for his life insurance agency.

He remembered my name and that I lived in Westborough. All I knew was that he looked familiar! We talked for a while. He was there because his friend's aunt had passed away and she was a long time member of Temple Emanuel. Mike didn't even belong to that temple. He belonged to the other Reform Temple in Worcester.

He asked me why I went to that temple since I lived in Westborough. I told him that my late husband was a good friend of the former Rabbi, so we joined there.

He then tried the lines "With or Without?" and "Do you or Don't You?" I had no idea what that meant. He said he thought that line wouldn't work.

He wanted to know if I was seeing someone.   I was thinking I was there for a yartzeit and I was being asked out on a date!

He asked for my business card and gave me his information. He wanted to know if I would like to go bike riding with him the next weekend. I thought to myself "Wow biking -- and he is in good shape!"

I drove home thinking what a strange way to meet someone -- at a temple at the time of a yartzeit for your late husband. I was curious; I looked him up on Linked-In. I found out he was 11 years older than I and also had graduated from University of Massachusetts.

I was busy that week with hosting Passover for fifteen people. I had a ton of left overs, and I saw that the forecast for the weekend was for rain. I decided to be adventurous and send him a message on LinkedIn inviting him to dinner on Thursday night. I figured that he worked in Westborough, and I had all that extra food. Why not?

I didn't hear from him right away, so I decided to try email. He responded immediately, "I would love to!"

Mike arrived carrying a beautiful bouquet of flowers. I set the table with all my food from Passover: turkey, brisket, chicken soup. He probably thought I cooked like that all the time.

I was clearing up and told him to make himself comfortable. The test was to see if he got along with my dog Schmutz! (She is a deal breaker.) Well he looked around, and saw the piano in the other room, and started playing. I knew right then he was **The One**. Active _and_ musical!

We dated all through the summer. One small problem; I had booked myself on a singles cruise in January for a trip in August.

I wanted to see the British Isles but I wasn't in the market for a single's cruise. I had already paid so I made the decision to just go. I could have fun with my friend and not look at it as a singles cruise. The other problem was Schmutzie. What do I do with my dog for two weeks? It was so expensive to board her.

I knew it was true love when Mike agreed to stay with Schmutzie at my house while I was away. He always joked with me after that he and Schmutzie bonded during that time!

The cruise was great, but I realized I wasn't interested in seeing anyone except Mike. I guess it was a good test.

CHAPTER 16

Losing my Job and Going Back to School

Graduation from Northeastern University,
Master's Program April 2012

IN SEPTEMBER, AFTER MY TRIP, I received an email from my dean, asking me to come into our Worcester campus to meet with Human Resources. Not good news! I saw the writing on the wall. I had seen enough people leave to know what that meant. I went into my office in Southborough and decided to clear out all my belongings-- just in case.

I drove into Worcester; the Dean was in the room with the HR person. Colleen said that she brought me in because I had missed quota in July and August. I was really surprised because I had missed quota by one in July and went on planned vacation in August (which was pre-approved) but was still expected to reach the same goal. I did exactly half the goal since I was away for two weeks. She said that it was unacceptable. I should have figured out a way to still achieve the goal.

I left upset but also very relieved – no more Becker! No more feeling like I wasn't worthy of respect. I decided to drive to Uhlman's Farm Ice Cream. I sat in the sun enjoying my ice cream -- free of Becker College.

I don't think it really hit me until I realized that I didn't have to wake up early for work the next morning. I was officially unemployed. The excitement didn't last too long. I was scared. I hadn't been unemployed for a long time. I worked straight from college. I had a few gaps but not for long. I kept thinking I will get something right away. I interview well and I have good experience.

Reality hit. I wasn't even getting interviews. What was wrong? I decided to focus my attention on graduate school. I had taken one class the previous spring, but hadn't taken anything that summer because of my trip. Now that I was unemployed, I had the time and devotion to dedicate myself to my studies. I took classes in Leadership and Non-Profit Management at Northeastern. It was once a week in Boston with the re-maining time on-line.

I loved being back at school -- except now I was the oldest in the class, and in some classes, the only American-born student. It was quite different from my undergraduate studies at University of Massachusetts or even the graduate certificate classes I had taken ten years prior at Northeastern.

It was a lot of reading and doing case studies. I would be doing a lot of papers, most of the time those were relegated to weekends. Overall, I loved it. I still looked for a full time job, but it wasn't my highest priority. I was trying to figure out what courses to take in the summer. I was thinking of taking on an internship and thought it would enable me to work in an environment I hadn't experienced in the past. But then I received an email from the administration announcing a new course for the summer. It was only for CPS students (College of Professional Studies) and was a way to expose us to studying abroad. Since it was a summer course, it would be just ten weeks, with eight on-line and two weeks in either Turkey or Italy. I went to the information session and saw the huge turn-out to enroll in the program. I was afraid I wasn't going to be chosen. I really wanted to study in Italy; I had been there a couple years prior and loved it. I really didn't have a burning desire to go to Turkey.

As it turned out, there wasn't a huge desire from the other students to go to Turkey either, so they offered only Italy. Also, many people who were interested never followed up; I was accepted into the program. I was very excited to be one of the twelve students to be enrolled in the course.

Our assignment was to do a project that combined our major with research in Italy. I decided to study the Leadership of the Jewish community of Italy and how it would survive in the future.

It was a remarkable trip, and I had the opportunity to not only study in Italy but also to explore Florence by living in an apartment and sharing experiences with a dozen other students from around the world. What an incredible adventure it was!

CHAPTER 17

Big Apple with Polly

Polly and I on the Rooftop looking out at the Hudson River, August 2012

In November 2011, my sisters Hope, Debra and I had decided to visit our Aunt Polly in New York City. She was our Mom's sister. She had never married and lived alone in NYC for over 50 years. For 30 or more years, she had lived in a third floor, one bedroom, rent controlled apartment near Lincoln Center. She paid around $300 a month. If you know New York prices, you know how much of a steal that was. Around ten years ago, she decided to buy a coop because she said that "one day I will be old and not able to walk up three flights of stairs."

She bought a coop on 74th Street and was on the fourth floor. Even though it had an elevator, she still would walk up the stairs.

Polly had worked most of her life in either the political arena or in state government. She was always volunteering for political campaigns or causes, visiting museums, watching plays or opera, or eating out with friends. She traveled extensively when she was younger-- until she was about 80.

We visited her because we hadn't seen her in a while, and we had heard from the front desk at the coop that she was complaining to them a lot.

We walked around the city for a while, then had lunch and said we would like to visit her apartment. Polly was very adamant that we didn't have to go there. However, we pushed to go; we felt she must be hiding something.

The apartment was a mess. Not only dirty but papers all over the nice hard wood floors and on the couches and tables. There was no place to sit. It was dangerous to walk around. We also wanted to talk to her about her future. Did she have a plan? Did she have a will? Power of attorney? We were nervous that at 84 she didn't have anything in place. If something happened, would there be anyone who would help her? Polly said she had friends that looked out for one-another. That didn't help in terms of her legal future. She did say that she was working with her attorney on her will, but hadn't done anything for a while. She said she needed to revise it.

We were afraid that if something happened, her friends wouldn't pull through. They were also older with families of their own. How would they be able to help out? We also had no idea where she would leave all her money. She was very generous with all her non-profits she was involved with. Would she give everything to Save the Whales or Planned Parenthood?

Polly had worked for over 60 years and had a very valuable apartment in New York City. She needed to have a proper will so that it would not just go to the State of New York. We got nowhere with her, she was very defensive.

We went home to Boston, feeling anxious. Right then she was ok, but what if she got worse; she was starting to show some signs of dementia.

My sisters and I decided to visit her more often and take on more responsibility for watching her. We started getting more calls from the front desk of her coop that she was calling the police saying that someone was stealing from her. I ended up visiting a couple more times. During the day she seemed ok; but my sisters and I could tell something was wrong. She was progressively getting worse. I went with her to the bank and we put everything in both of our names. It was a huge struggle. Luckily she liked the customer service person at the bank and he and I met a few other times. He helped convince her that I can take care of her bills so she didn't have to worry anymore about it. It was a huge step. Suddenly I was in charge of all her bills and organizing her paperwork.

In the summer of 2012, we decided that we should look into Independent Living facilities. She was getting very scattered during the day and at night very paranoid. We thought that with fewer things to look after, things might be better. She would also be interacting with more people.

We found a beautiful place on West 86th Street near the Hudson. At first she was excited about the idea. Then she was very nervous; she wanted to back out of the entire thing.

Finally, on Labor Day, we moved her to her new place. We kept her coop just in case. She didn't like the people. They weren't friendly or not smart enough or were too deaf. Whatever she could complain about, she would. She liked the food but then complained that she was gaining weight. She would start walking back to her old apartment to check on the mail and would walk around the city a lot because she was bored (her new place was an "open" facility.)

We started getting phone calls from the staff that she was walking around at night in her tights. It wasn't safe. What could we do? We were 4 ½ hours away and she was 84!

The worst call came in October. She was being taken to the hospital in the middle of the night. They found a kitchen knife in her apartment under her mattress. She was accusing people there of stealing. The facility was treating her like a criminal, she said.

They told her that she was not fit to live there. She needed to have constant supervision. She was a threat not only to herself but to others.

We were desperate. What could we do? Polly mentioned she would be willing to move to Boston to be closer to us. So we started looking into places near us. It was a huge job looking at different facilities. The place where she was living was giving her only a month to make a new living arrangement. Living in Boston would be easier for us to keep in touch with her, but she would be bored. She loved New York. All of her friends were there. We also looked at facilities in New York City. We had the opportunity to meet a geriatric health care professional who was at a conference in Marlborough but based in New York City. She was a God send. We decided to hire her, and she helped us decide what to do. We had only a few weeks before we had to move her.

We ultimately decided to move Polly back to her own apartment -- but with supervision. She absolutely hated it. She had never had roommates or live-in companions, so this was infringing on her freedom!

We got calls constantly that they were stealing from her. Nancy (the social worker) was helpful meeting with Polly and hiring the aides. I got calls from her bank that someone was stealing from her. I had to help her get out of that financial mess. This time someone was actually stealing from her. One of the aides forged her signature and wrote a check to herself as a "Holiday Bonus" for $500.

Not only was Polly deteriorating mentally, but physically she was not doing well either. She had colitis years ago, and it was coming back. It was getting worse and she was constantly running. We started getting calls that she was going to the hospital because of her dehydration.

From April through June Polly rapidly deteriorated. She had gotten an infection in the hospital, and when she was in rehab she hardly ate so she had to go immediately back to the hospital. Debra, Hope, and I visited her in May. I knew that it would probably be the last time we would see her.

CHAPTER 18

End of Schmutz

Schmutz 1999- 2012

THIS IS A POST THAT I put into my blog about Schmutz. I felt it deserved to be in the blog about Steve because the dog was really Steve's love. I did love her but not nearly as much as Steve did.

September 4, 2012-- It has been a while since I had posted. Today I had to put Schmutzie to sleep. She was 13 1/2 -- it was a very difficult decision. For the past thirteen years she had been a great dog. However, she was a lot like Marley (in the book or movie). Schmutz was a very destructive dog; she ruined two sofas, peed on more floors and rugs than I can count, and even ruined a door (scratching it when she was anxious) However, she was also very lovable. She was there when I lost my Mom, Steve and Dad. She had a sense when something was wrong. She would lie very still and look up at me and convey that "we can make it."

Over the past 3 1/2 years she had been a real support. I knew if I dated someone, Schmutzie had better like them. If she didn't, watch out! For the past year and a half, I had been seeing Mike. She really bonded with him, so I guess he is a keeper! Mike and I both went to the vet yesterday. We both noticed that she had been having more and more difficulty walking. She was collapsing on the driveway and couldn't do stairs anymore. I knew that she was going to get progressively worse. While I was walking her yesterday, she stumbled a couple of times and she looked up at me. It was like she was saying, "It is time."

We decided to put her down yesterday because we knew it was the right time. She was having a harder and harder time walking and we didn't want her to suffer more. Schmutzie really was part of not just my family but whoever got to know her. Hopefully she is with Steve and they are walking around heaven together! We love you Schmutzie and we miss you! Beth

I knew that as soon as we put Schmutzie down, we would have to start working on the house. So many times over the years I had wanted to fix something or replace a piece of furniture, but thought that the dog would just ruin it, so I didn't bother.

Throughout the time that I was dealing with my aunt, unemployment, and Schmutzie, Mike kept me positive. After I came back from the British Islands, I knew that it was serious. It was also too soon to think about moving in together. He did want to get out of his apartment in Worcester. Instead of moving in right away, he moved into an apartment in Marlborough, above his office at work. Even though we spent so much time together, I needed to de-clutter or "De-schmutz" my house.

A lot of the year was spent decluttering or fixing the house. I would get rid of things and realize there was so much more to go! I hadn't done any real work on the house for so long because I thought that Schmutz would just ruin it.

When the workmen were working on the house, Mike and I asked them to take down Schmutzie's dog house. We both helped take it down and decided to keep the sign that said "Schmutz". We buried her ashes in the backyard in a huge hole she had dug when she was a puppy near a big rock in the middle of the yard. I decided to plant a rosebush. I thought it was very significant because she was beautiful -- but had a sharp edge to her.

We started the renovations by getting rid of the rugs in the extra bedrooms. We noticed that it would smell like dog when it was humid and it was just not worth keeping them. It was difficult to do because I had so much "stuff" in the rooms that it just felt impossible. How did I accumulate so much over the years?

The next project was to paint the walls. I had plain white walls throughout the house. I don't know why I was hesitant to have color in the rooms. Was I afraid I would get sick of the color? What if I didn't like it? We repainted all the rooms upstairs and the hallways. It was amazing. The only problem was when they took out the window air conditioner in my bedroom, they noticed that it had leaked and created mold in the wall. They had to get rid of all the mold in the wall and get a new window. This opened up a can of worms for us. Why should they fix only one window? All the windows were old and inefficient. The next thing I knew, we were replacing all the windows in the house!

Little by little we ended up fixing the entire house. We installed a new roof, put down a new floor in the dining room (Schmutzie ruined the floor), and refinished the basement. The more we worked, the more we uncluttered and the more likely that there would be room for Mike move in.

CHAPTER 19

Engagement Rings
and Wedding Bells

Beth and Michael Whitman's Wedding June 2, 2013

In September 2012, Mike and I planned a trip to Vermont. I knew it was going to be the "big weekend", but I didn't know any details. It was a beautiful resort up in Champlain Valley. One of Mike's friends recommended the place. We drove up on Friday and stopped along the way for lunch in a beautiful college town.

We got to the resort and saw a wedding in progress. We tried to check in without getting in the way. We went into our room and found champagne, strawberries and chocolate. It was so romantic.

We walked around the gorgeous grounds and took pictures near the lake. It was such an ideal area. We had a nice dinner, and the next day we planned to go for a bike ride around the town. It was cold and raw, but we decided to go anyway. We had our windbreakers. Mine wasn't too warm, so Mike offered me his to use. I noticed that there was a box in the pocket, but didn't say anything. We rode, but since it was cold and rainy, it wasn't the time to "pop the question."

We came back and went on a boat ride around the lake. It was such a beautiful lake, but the weather was still not cooperating. We came back to our room and dressed for dinner at the fancy restaurant on the property. We were seated near this very noisy group. Mike was very agitated. He asked the waiter if we could switch. Normally it didn't bother him, but it did that evening; the restaurant was empty, so they didn't mind.

We ordered our meals and right before they were ready to serve our salads, he took out the ring. He motioned to the wait staff to hold up for a few seconds. He got down on his knee and proposed. It was a beautiful ring, but more importantly, I was so excited to be engaged to Mike. The waiters came over with champagne and took pictures of us. It was such an amazing evening. The food was incredible. I kept on looking at the ring and smiling up at Mike.

The next day we had an amazing brunch at the inn and then drove to Burlington, Vermont and visited my favorite place: "Ben and Jerry's." After taste testing the ice cream, we drove back through western Mass. Mike wanted to see one of his old clients. Lou was so appreciative for the help that Mike had given over the years that he gave him a big check (which paid for not only the ring but the weekend) Mike wanted me to meet Lou because he meant so much to him. It was a great visit and very meaningful for Mike.

We called my sisters and Mike's parents and his kids. They were all thrilled. I called a couple of friends, but it was too much to tell everyone. I knew this was a time for Facebook. I knew it would be difficult, but the one person I wanted to tell was Steve's Mom, who I affectionately called "Other Mom." I had become so close with her over the years. She had met Mike a couple of times in Westborough and in Sarasota, but I knew it would be difficult to tell her I was getting remarried. She was thrilled. "Other Mom" was very glad that I had called her and that she didn't hear it through Facebook first!

Speaking of Facebook, I had so many likes and comments, in the hundreds, it shut down my account! I tried to get onto Facebook and it wasn't allowing me access. People were thrilled and excited that I had gotten engaged and had moved on in my life.

In October, Mike decided to move in. He had moved to Marlborough from his old apartment in Worcester, but it had been temporary. We knew he would eventually move into the house, but we needed to make room for him and his furniture.

I had done some decluttering before, but we needed to get rid of a lot more things now that he was becoming part of my life.

Mike was really helpful in getting me to de clutter the house. When I was doubtful about the process he would just say "Get Rid of it" and signaled as if he was an umpire throwing someone out after striking out.

Each room was torture to go through. Not everything had sentimental value, but it was years of accumulation. I just froze when I would look at another project to start.

Before Mike moved into the house, I needed to get rid a lot of "stuff" so there would be room for him. It wasn't just the physical stuff that was hard to get rid of, but also the psychological. Letting go of things was letting go of Steve and letting myself move on. I had to be ready. It was a huge process. I was married to Steve for close to 18 years, and had known him for close to 21.

I knew I was getting there when I decided to take all the pictures off the mantel. I had so many pictures from our wedding, trips, and our family. I just couldn't throw them away. I decided to make a memory box for Steve. I put our ketubah (Jewish marriage agreement), some wedding pictures, and various favorite pictures into the box. I also put the two binders of cards that kids created in Steve's memory. I added posters from his concerts that he performed and also his favorite tee shirts (Grateful Dead, youth group tee shirts and various other musicians) I took out the pictures from a collage and put in new pictures from me and Mike. It was very significant. I put all that up in the attic safe and it is still in my possession, but not there in front of me all the time.

From the summer of 2012 through June 2013, we decluttered the house. We also fixed things throughout the house. Steve and I had done some maintenance over the years on the house, but there was still a lot of work to be done. We always put things off because there was always tension trying to make decisions on every aspect of the project.

Over that year we fixed everything from the roof and attic to the basement; we completely redid the house. Mike helped me push through. Everything I had put off for years because it was too hard to deal with at the time. I finally felt like I was getting my life back because I wasn't drowning in my stuff. I knew that if I was going to succeed, I needed to keep as organized as I could. I set up huge file cabinets in my office so I could be on top of all my paperwork. I used Mike's grandmother's credenza for my office instead of for my china. I put all my office supplies and paper in there. Where all the silverware would normally be, I put all the pens and pencils. I knew that the more time I spent on organizing, the more I would feel in control of my life.

Planning the wedding was much different from 1991. I didn't want the huge wedding. When Steve and I got married we had 175 people. We had it at my temple with a big band and caterer. I didn't want anything like that. We both wanted to keep it small.

We decided to invite only immediate family and very close friends. No cousins. Even though I only had a few first cousins, Mike had tons. If we had decided to open it up it would have tripled the size of the wedding. We ended up having 36 people.

During the months before the wedding, we met with the Rabbi to create a service that we both liked. At first it just wasn't working. All the readings and ideas she suggested weren't resonating. One day I asked her if we could add music. We invited the cantorial soloist to participate in the wedding ceremony. All of a sudden we both were excited about the ceremony. That was the missing link.

The cantorial soloist was extremely talented. She played the guitar, flute, and piano. We incorporated all three instruments into the service and the processional. Aside from the wedding ceremony, we wanted to have a special Shabbat service on the Friday night. We worked with the cantorial soloist and created a Jazz Shabbat. I played guitar for a couple of songs, and Mike played piano for a couple. It was a really fun service to create.

We decided to have the wedding reception at Romaine's restaurant in Northborough. We had gone there after I came back from Italy and loved the food. They had a great room in the back that would be perfect for a reception. We asked one of Mike's friends to play keyboard, and he had another friend who played bass. It was coming together.

I looked around at bridal shops and everything was really for "twenty something" brides. Dresses were either too frilly or short. Nothing was for a "forty something" bride. I remember going into David's Bridal, giving a description of what I wanted and finding nothing that I liked. My sister Hope said "Why don't you wear Debra's gown?" I first said no. I wanted my own; then I went over to her house. The gown I was describing to the woman at David's Bridal was my sister's gown. It was sophisticated and elegant. I tried it on and it fit perfectly.

We decided to plan a wedding weekend. Friday night we wanted our families to meet and spend a little time together at dinner. Then we could all go to the temple for services. Well, it didn't happen that way. Mike's Dad made reservations ahead of time, and they were arriving later than we thought. I was hoping that they would be able to make it, and I was upset when I found out that they just wanted to relax that evening after a hectic flight.

Instead we had close to 30 friends and my family over for dinner. It was a really beautiful evening and everyone ate outside. We figured we couldn't invite all our friends for the wedding, so we should have them over for either dinner or to the service. It was a great evening; I remember playing one of the songs at the service *Lecha Dodi* (the Sabbath bride), and stood in the back as if I was the Sabbath bride coming into the service.

The next day we spent with Mike's family. They came in from Florida, and his sister came in from South Carolina. Mike's parents were celebrating their 60th anniversary, so we decided to go out the night before to celebrate. We had a picture from their 50th anniversary and put it on the cake. It was wonderful spending the evening with Mike's family (my new family)

The morning of the wedding, I wanted Mike out of the house. He had brunch with his parents and his sister, while I got my hair and make-up done. I had my hairdresser come to the house. I had gone to her for years, so she was happy to come over. She texted me that she was coming early; she would be there in 15 minutes. There went my leisurely day!

She arrived with her tools—and her 6 month old puppy. I was horrified. Here I was getting married in a few hours and she had the nerve to come with a puppy. I asked her to put it outside, but she insisted that the dog was very well trained and could stay inside.

It wasn't. The dog kept on pulling and distracting her. The "piece de resistance" was when Suzanne asked me for some styling moose because she had forgotten hers. I went upstairs and when I returned, there was a "present for me;" The dog had pooped in my dining room. I was exasperated. She just said "Don't worry, I will clean it up." (*I was thinking; of course you will!*) I told her to take the dog outside; I couldn't keep the dog in the house anymore. Finally she finished my hair and left. I was so upset; I didn't even like my hair!

Then it was time for Michelle to do my makeup. She was running late. I was already agitated, so waiting around didn't help. She came about 15 minutes late but brought beautiful flowers. It was so nice of her. She put on soothing music and started working on the makeup. She was totally the opposite from my hairdresser. She was calming and doing anything she could to help me get ready. I put on my gown and she helped me with the veil and made me feel more relaxed. I was almost ready when Mike blasted into the house. "I have to take a quick shower and I will be done soon" I couldn't believe how he waited until the last minute to get ready. I heard him upstairs swearing. He couldn't do the buttons for the tux. I finally said I have to get to the temple because the photographer was due soon. I went ahead without him; a few minutes later he came in. It worked out fine because the photographer always takes a million pictures of the bride.

The ceremony was incredible. The cantorial soloist played a classical piece on the flute as Mike walked down the aisle with his parents. When I walked in with my two sisters, she was playing a Jewish song on the guitar.

It was perfect. The Rabbi and Cantor did an amazing job. At the end of the ceremony, they played some Hora music and we all started dancing around the sanctuary. We knew that it wouldn't be appropriate in the restaurant, but after our ceremony it worked out perfectly. Mike's friends lifted us up on chairs, and everyone was dancing around us. It was amazing.

We took pictures with our families. I also asked for a picture of me with "Other Mom and Dad;" It was really special for me. They were very glad to be there with the families. Without having my own parents, I now had two sets of in-laws.

The reception was a lot of fun. Having just a small group made it really intimate. The musicians were great. They asked Mike to play his signature song *A Train* and he asked me to sing something. I didn't know any jazz, so I decided to sing *Summertime*. I didn't really know the words, but I just had everyone singing along for the chorus.

We had decided to wait a couple of weeks to go on our honeymoon; Mike's parents were going to stay that week and go to the Whitman family reunion the next weekend. It turned out to be too much for them, so they actually stayed only through Monday. But it was an incredible weekend.

The reunion was fun. I now knew why we hadn't included first cousins on the guest list. Mike's father was one of eight children; there were close to 50 people at the reunion. We had one entire tier leftover from the wedding cake, so we took it to the party and shared it with the family. So in fact they *were* part of the wedding.

Before going off to Hawaii, I went down to New York with Debra and Hope to visit Polly in the hospital. She was definitely going downhill fast. I knew this would probably be our last visit. She had gotten an infection when she was at the hospital earlier in the spring and never fully recovered. She recognized us, but was very unresponsive. It was so hard to see this woman who had been so full of energy all of her life just lying in the hospital.

On a beautiful day the next week, Mike and I decided to go on a short bike ride around the neighborhood. I usually bike behind him because I hate to worry if he is behind me or not. This time I went in front because his hip was bothering him a bit and he didn't want to slow me down.

I decided after each big turn (we did a big loop) to stop to make sure he was ok. The third loop was on a hill, so I didn't stop the momentum. I was half way up the hill when someone in a car stopped and asked if I was biking with someone. I said that I was biking with my husband. She said that he had wiped out on the sand a mile back

I raced back to the spot she mentioned. I was terrified to see him injured. When I got there, he wasn't on the ground. Someone in a pick-up truck was yelling out to me "I am in here." Luckily there were good Samaritans who saw him, one guy put the bike in his truck and assisted Mike into his truck.

Mike had wiped out on the sand. His face was bloodied, his glasses broken and his shoulder, elbow and hip were scraped. The guy drove us back to the house. He knew I was too shaken up to bike back, so he threw my bike in the back with Mike's.

One of the bystanders said to me. "Make sure that he stays awake. You don't want him to lose consciousness." Mike said that he was starving, so I made him peanut butter and jelly sandwiches. He devoured them and we drove to the hospital. He looked horrible and he was extremely sore. I kept on thinking I was glad it hadn't happened before the wedding. He would have looked all beaten up for the wedding pictures.

He had an extremely nice nurse and doctor; they took x-rays and remarkably he hadn't broken any bones. The problem was we were leaving for Hawaii in a week and he wouldn't be too comfortable on that long plane ride.

I had always wanted to go to Hawaii, but it was such a long expensive trip so it was always on the bucket list of places to go "sometime." A few years back I had joined a travel club to travel weeks at a discounted rate. Instead of owning a time share, I paid for one to two weeks a year. It has been a great investment since we were able to use it all around the country. At a whim I looked to see if they had anything in Hawaii, and they had a place in Kawaii. I was so excited. Mike had gone there on a business trip but wanted to go back for a personal trip. Since it was part of my travel club and I also had a lot of frequent flyer miles, the trip was a lot less expensive than we had thought.

Our place was on the East coast of Kawaii -- right on the water. It was a really long flight, but went extremely well. I brought a lot of snacks along and had a lot to read (mainly travel books about Hawaii)

The first morning we went to a short introductory meeting for guests. This was something new to us. They had a real song and dance show to promote their day excursions. They had raffles as well. I am notorious for winning raffle prizes, so when they called my name, I was excited but not surprised. We won a day-long cruise. It was "buy one cruise and get one free." I was thrilled. We spent the rest of the day choosing our excursions for the remainder of the week.

One of the good things about our place was that it had a full kitchen, so throughout the week we made breakfast smoothies with our fresh fruit and sandwiches for the beach. We ate out most nights, and took any leftovers back to our place. We saved a ton of money on meals.

One day we rented bikes to explore the island. They had a short bike trail and one speed bikes-- which was fine. I hadn't ridden one of those in decades! The end of the trail just ended without any sign. Mike saw that there was a small dirt path and proceeded right down the hill. I was in back of him yelling, "That isn't part of the trail." He yelled back "be adventurous." It got narrow and kind of steep downhill. There were no brakes on the bike and I had forgotten how to stop. I kind of kicked my feet out and scraped my legs on the brush to slow myself down. At the bottom of the hill, there was a small brook; I tripped and twisted my ankle. I was shouting to Mike to stop and he said "What is the problem? It is beautiful here!"

That was our first fight as a married couple. We cut through fields and climbed over fences until we found a paved road. Mike now knew that he was the adventurous one, and that I was much more cautious. I was also thinking that he was still healing from his bike accident, so I was very hesitant to take chances. Since then, we always discuss a ride ahead of time; if there is a questionable route, we talk about it before he starts riding. Luckily we hadn't been hurt, but I had to remember that he is like a little kid on his bike, nothing stops him!

The rest of our vacation was amazing. We went on boat rides, van rides touring the island, enjoyed luaus and visited many beautiful sites throughout the island. The best part was that I was with my new husband who was able to not only keep up with me, but even push me to do more physically challenging things.

Hawaii Honeymoon, June 2013

CHAPTER 20

Losing Polly

DURING OUR HONEYMOON I GOT a text from my sister Debra, saying that my Aunt Polly had passed away on June 25th. She was 85. It was sad to see how fast she had declined. I was glad that I had been able to see her before I left for Hawaii.

My sisters and I had discussed before I left whether I should cancel my trip if she passed. They both said that I should go; I had been able to see her recently. She was much more than just an aunt to me; I was very close to her. She was a mentor to me in many ways.

After I got back from Hawaii, my sisters and I took a bus down to NYC to handle the last details. We decided to sell the coop to her neighbors; they had a connecting wall so they could expand their own apartment and have a majority of the fourth floor. It was actually a good solution for all of us. We didn't have to worry about selling it on the market and renovating it (which it needed badly), and they really needed more space for their growing three girls.

We had the daunting task of packing up all of her stuff. She had so many things and the problem was that we didn't want to take anything big home with us. We donated a lot of clothes, dishes and furniture. We knew some of the items would have been worth something, but it was just too much work to move them. One of Hope's friends was in NY and offered to take the paintings back in her car.

My aunt had wanted to be cremated. The perfect place for her ashes would have been Central Park, since she had lived near the park for 30 plus years, but it was illegal to pour ashes in the park. We decided to go to Ellis Island. Our grandmother had come over from Poland to Ellis Island, so we thought it was appropriate. They also had a very nice garden near the water so we had a small ceremony there. We debated about doing more. Her friends wanted us to do a memorial service, but not during the summer. At first we weren't going to do it, but those friends had been there for her for decades, so it was important. She deserved a nice memorial.

In September we decided to have a memorial service at a non-profit agency down the street from my aunt's co-op. We got nice bagels and cream cheese and created a video collage of pictures of my aunt through the years. The nicest part of the day was when each person (over 40 people) shared a short story about their relationship with Polly. I only wish we had video-taped the event. Some of the stories were amazing. Polly had worked on political campaigns from Kennedy to Obama, had gone to concerts and operas, and had worked in correctional facilities and with volunteer groups.

Everyone had a fascinating story to share about Polly and we learned many wonderful things about her. It was a great tribute to an amazing woman.

CHAPTER 21

Starting Over from Scratch

AFTER RETURNING FROM HAWAII AND dealing with my aunt's estate, I felt very alone -- but I also felt free from responsibilities. For years I had been dealing with my Dad and my aunt's declining health. Suddenly, I wasn't paying someone else's bills, taking someone to doctors' appointments, or visiting them in the hospital.

I was becoming very discouraged about my job search. I thought that since I had just earned my master's degree, I would have more opportunities. I was getting very frustrated; I would get interviews but then they chose another candidate. I was either overqualified for some non-profit jobs, or underqualified for fundraising jobs because I hadn't raised enough money at Northeastern.

Mike is the great networker; he told me that he met someone at a meeting who was looking for sales people for promotional products. I wasn't thrilled but thought I could do it; I was very social and I loved "chatkas" (knick-knacks). I did all the right things in terms of marketing. I wrote a newsletter, created a Facebook page, and went to networking events. I just had a hard time getting on the phone and calling people. I tried for several months, but nothing clicked. I just had no passion to sell promotional products.

I went to a seminar by Jewish Vocational Service for women job seekers. It was an eight week course. It wasn't about techniques, but about writing goals and establishing accountability. I liked the group, and it was helpful. During that time I had a very promising couple of interviews. I was so close -- then they said that they had gone with another candidate. I was so frustrated.

I read a few books about motivation and job hunting for mid- career professionals. I was just stuck.

Mike was so supportive and understanding, but I still felt that nothing would ever turn around. He kept telling me that I had grown so much in the past few months and that I shouldn't get discouraged. For me, being unemployed for so long was a real loss. I was very depressed; I had no identity. For years I had been the Hillel Director. I loved working with students and making a difference in their lives. I hated going to any family or social events because they would ask me the dreaded question, "What do you do?" I would just cringe.

CHAPTER 22

As the Stomach Turns...

THROUGHOUT THE YEAR I WAS began experimenting with my cooking. When I was married to Steve, I had rarely cooked. Steve was the chef, and I was the sous-chef. Also, I made food for Hillel and was rarely at home at the same time as Steve.

Living with Mike was very different. I worked closer to home so there wasn't the long commute from Boston. Also, Mike liked my cooking. We liked eating together at home. Making dinner was more of an event. He was so appreciative of the home cooked meals; it made me want to cook and try out new recipes.

The problem was Mike loved the different foods that I created but some just didn't agree with his stomach. I would make some vegetarian dishes like eggplant parmigiana or Moroccan tagine and he would eat a ton of it, but then his acid reflux would kick in. I read about all the benefits of juicing, but the fiber would not agree with him.

It all came to a head when we had a 60th birthday party for him. We decided to have it catered by El Basha (Mediterranean food), and I bought a deadly chocolate cake and made some other decadent desserts. We both ate a lot. The next morning Mike woke up with his throat feeling really restricted; when he swallowed it would hurt not only his throat but in his chest.

Normally, he would have taken something, but he felt something else must be going on. We decided to go to a Medi-Clinic. After doing a couple of tests, they concluded that since he was 60, had a history of high cholesterol, and had pain in his chest, that we shouldn't take a chance. They rushed him to the hospital in an ambulance.

I drove in my car behind the ambulance and kept thinking, "This can't be happening. I can't lose Mike too! "

We got to the hospital and they put him in a room right away. They tested him for a heart attack (which was negative) and gave him some antacid medication. They wouldn't let him leave because they had to test people two times every six hours. So we had to stay at the hospital all day on his 60th Birthday.

They didn't do any other tests so we had no idea what was causing him so much discomfort. Mike was a good sport; he kept asking the nurses if he could at least get a TV in his room so he could watch the Patriots game. They finally moved him, but the Patriots lost in the end.

We finally went home at 6pm. They just told him to set up an appointment with his primary care doctor and get an endoscopy to test what was going on in his stomach.

That Monday he had the procedure, they told him he had GERD (Gastroesophageal Reflux Disease) and told him what not to eat. We looked at the list, he was already doing many of the recommendations: No fried foods, no greasy foods, stay away from caffeine or spicy foods.

They also gave him an over-the-counter prescription to take for a month. He was fed up; he felt like it was just masking the symptoms. He still didn't know why he was having stomach problems and what foods he could eat.

One day when he was getting a massage, his therapist recommended that he go to the nutritionist across the hall from her office. Mike was tired of having to guess what to eat and just couldn't deal with medications anymore.

That January, Mike went to the nutritionist she recommended. He insisted that I go with him. He knew I made all the food, and he wanted me to be there for support.

Mike went twice a month and was given a special diet called GAP (Gut and Psychology) diet. We had no idea why she picked the diet, but she said that she needed to rebuild his stomach lining.

The first couple of weeks were extremely difficult. All he ate was soup. At first Mike liked it because he loves chicken soup. But having it for breakfast, lunch and dinner for days in a row got old fast.

Gradually, over the next few months she increased the foods he could eat, but still little or no carbs. The only carbs were vegetables. Mike lost weight right away (having no carbs really does get rid of the wheat belly), but he was always hungry.

In February, I was watching the Biggest Loser and was so inspired by the stories. I loved seeing people being totally transformed through diet and exercise. I said to myself I would like to do something like that which motivates people and explores their deeper reasons for needing to lose weight.

One day while I was searching the Internet for yet another job opportunity, I saw an advertisement that interested me. It was for an on-line certificate program in nutritional counseling. It was a year-long program with an emphasis on nutrition, building a health coaching business, and developing counseling skills. This year-long program would be a great opportunity for me. I loved learning about different nutritional diets, and I was interested in counseling.

I decided in February to enroll. I loved it. Institute for Integrative Nutrition was just what I was looking for. There were no long reading assignments; everything was online video or audio lectures. They had experts in the field and a lot of hands-on training in counseling.

There was part of me wondering "why am I going back to school again?" I had just finished my masters and I realized I wasn't finding a fulfilling career. I wanted to make a difference in people's lives around their health.

It was interesting to go to Mike's nutritionist while I was in my certificate program. What I realized was that I was glad I was studying to be a health coach vs a nutritionist or dietitian.

What was missing from the nutritionist sessions was what the school called "bio-individuality". She chose a diet but was not adapting it to meet Mike's specific needs.

Mike had high cholesterol (family background). The diet was very high in protein and fat. A couple of months into the diet, he was feeling a lot better but he was nervous about his cholesterol. He had his doctor run a cholesterol test. The doctor and Mike were both shocked. Mike's good cholesterol (HDL) had gone up 10 points, but the bad number (LDL) had gone up over 100 points. The doctor was alarmed, but the nutritionist felt he shouldn't be concerned, as long as his HDL was going up. She showed Mike some articles that dismissed the importance of cholesterol.

Mike decided to listen to his doctor. The doctor first recommended cholesterol medicine, but Mike refused. He didn't want to go that route. So he suggested that Mike meet with the practice's dietician on staff. Mike figured there was nothing to lose. The good part was that it would be covered by his health insurance (which the other nutritionist was not).

This dietitian looked at his diet and was shocked. She said he was starving himself on this diet. She immediately put him on a gluten-free diet. Instead of high fat yogurt, she recommended a 2 percent fat version. Mike was so thrilled to be able to have gluten-free cereal. He was finally feeling more satisfied. I started gathering tons of recipes for gluten-free meals and desserts.

He also knew that if he ate something with too much sugar that it would bother him. Eventually, Mike noticed that the dairy products were bothering him more. The dietician cut out the yogurt and dairy. He started having more almond milk and making "Milk shakes" with almond milk, fruit, and chocolate or peanut butter. I was learning more about nutrition from dealing with Mike's food issues than I was in my classes. He was my ideal client.

CHAPTER 23

Creating Bouncing Back

HALF WAY THROUGH THE PROGRAM with Institute for Integrative Nutrition, we were able to start meeting with clients and establishing our business. During those months we practiced doing health histories on other students. At first it was really challenging, but after a while I became better at listening and making possible recommendations, not giving outright advice.

I realized I really enjoyed it! During one of the health histories, one of the students said it is amazing how I had just bounced back after all I had gone through. That name stuck. I said to her "I think I want to call my business "Bouncing Back"

Institute for Integrative Nutrition set up a website and offered free business cards. I decided to join the local chamber of commerce in order to network and promote my new business. I also noticed a meet up for entrepreneurial women. I loved the idea of networking and promoting my business. I worked with someone to update my website to make it more personalized.

What I realized was that I was doing everything right in terms of marketing, but I wasn't signing any clients. I also felt that it was hard to describe what I did. I had this pre-conceived notion that people wouldn't want to pay so much for a health coach.

Over the past year, I have offered a variety of programs from cleanses to detoxes. During these programs, I worked with the groups to not only lose weight and inches, but also gain energy and sleep. For the individual clients, it gave people a chance to work one-on-one and learn valuable tips for not only weight loss, but other issues they are addressing in their lives. My culinary expertise was also unleashed when I was able to offer cooking classes to groups who wanted to learn how to make healthy meals.

While writing this book I realized that my emphasis shifted from being just a nutritional coach to being a more holistic health coach. When discussing my journey from loss to rejuvenation, I realized there was a great need for my services in the world. There are many nutritionists or dieticians, but not many who have the added expertise about dealing with loss.

CHAPTER 24

Bouncing Back after a Fall

Mike and I in Lake Tahoe, September 2014

IN SEPTEMBER OF 2014, MIKE and I went on a vacation to Lake Tahoe. I saw a show on HGTV that promoted the area and fell in love with it. They were highlighting the biking, hiking, and sight-seeing around the lake. Lake Tahoe was also affiliated with our travel club. When I booked online, I saw that there was a charity bike ride around Lake Tahoe during our vacation week. It was 72 miles, with an alternative of 36 miles with a boat ride. It was scheduled for the second day of our vacation. We were so excited; I rented bikes and made sure we had a car that could transport bikes.

When we arrived, we had a wonderful dinner and then bought tons of groceries for the week. With Mike's food sensitivities, it was a God-send to have a kitchen.

The next day we picked up our bikes and decided to try a ride around the area. We wanted to feel comfortable with the clips and the shifting. On our ride we saw a nice marina and some neighborhoods around the lake. On the way back I was biking, but then I don't remember…

The next thing I knew someone was asking me "Do you know where you are? Do you know what happened?" I looked up and saw bright lights and a hallway. Then I was in a hospital room. What had happened?

Mike was in the room looking extremely anxious. I asked him what had happened and he told me that I had fallen on the road and that someone saw me fall. Another person had found him a little bit farther down the road

The "Guardian Angel" held my head in her lap and kept saying to Mike, "She is alive; she just is not responsive." I was unconscious for about 15 – 20 minutes. I had fallen and hit my head and hurt my shoulder, but there were no other obvious injuries.

An ambulance rushed me to the hospital. Mike must have called the bike rental place to pick up the bikes. I was in the hospital for 24 hours. They did every type of test: MRI, X-rays on my shoulder, etc.

They kept asking me questions," Do you know where you are? Who is the president?" At night the monitor kept going off. They told me my heart rate was really low and had hit 35 beats a minute. I have a low heart rate normally, but this was unusually low.

They were concerned, but I was finally allowed to leave with a huge list of things I shouldn't do, since I had had a concussion. No TV or computer and no biking for at least 6 weeks. There went the vacation.

I was so bummed. The bike ride was out because I was in the hospital, but extra bike trips around the lake were out as well.

Mike didn't want me to exert myself; he wanted to take care of me. Then I realized I hadn't been a patient in a hospital since I had had my tonsils out when I was just seven.

I was always the caretaker -- never the patient. I didn't want to be taken care of. I tried to help, but Mike stopped me. It was very frustrating. I was feeling fine for the most part and didn't want to be dependent.

I remember trying to empty the dishwasher and got really dizzy. The change from going up and down was bothering me.

It finally made me realize that I needed to take better care of myself.

Surprisingly, the week went really well. We planned new things to do over the vacation and had a great time. Every time I tried to push too much, I realized it was ok to step back and allow myself to heal.

I tried to *Bounce Back* too fast. Over the next two weeks, we went to many more doctor's appointments. I went to a cardiologist because of their concern about my low heart rate. They had me wear a monitor for a full day and track my activity. It was normal. They concluded that my heart rate could have been abnormal because of the elevation of Lake Tahoe or the environment of the hospital.

Another doctor tested my brain activity to make sure everything was ok. To make sure it was a one-time occurrence and not a seizure.

After an EKG, my primary care doctor called to report that the test came back abnormal. I was freaking out. "What was the matter with me? Was it a tumor or was I susceptible to seizures?"

They wanted me to see a neurologist. They referred me to a doctor in Framingham. I called and they said that they couldn't see me for another 6 weeks. The secretary was rude; she practically laughed at me when I said I wanted something that week.

I called the referral office again and asked for another name. They had another doctor in my town; I called and they had a cancellation. They could see me the following day. I was relieved that I could see someone right away.

The doctor seemed very young but was very professional and personable. He looked at the chart and said that it did show abnormalities, but with my history he did not see that it was a recurring thing. He said that if he diagnosed it as a seizure I wouldn't be able to drive for six months.

He asked me how I was feeling and if I had any more symptoms. I had been feeling much better.

He said that the abnormality was due to the concussion and told me to continue to stay off the bike for a few more weeks, and if anything changed, to call him right away.

All the tests were coming back normal.

I asked my doctor to prescribe physical therapy for my shoulder because I wanted to strengthen it right way and not have trouble long- term. I went for six weeks; it was a great help. She gave me some new exercises, adapted some of my regular ones for the shoulder, and told me not to push too hard.

It was tough getting back to classes at my gym. I felt very dizzy doing yoga, exercises on the stability ball, or any type of balance work.

Eventually I felt better and didn't even think about my shoulder or my dizziness anymore.

CHAPTER 25
Creating a New Life

EVEN THOUGH I FELT THAT my life was getting back to normal, I was getting very discouraged that my business was not growing.

I felt like I would never get clients. I started doubting myself and my knowledge. Was I doing the right thing?

Mike was so supportive of me. He kept saying that it is very difficult to build a business. I was always comparing myself to the other graduates who already had a lot of clients.

I was repeatedly saying to myself, "I am doing everything right? Why am I not getting clients?" I was realizing that my self- doubt had been a recurring theme throughout my life. Did I know enough? Am I good enough?

So many times in my life I would get so close to goal then get afraid and back off. I decided to do an extra year of my program to perfect my business skills. But I realized that I was in the same boat as a lot of other graduates.

I actually was further along in my marketing than the others. Also some had "Free clients" but not paying clients. That was reassuring, but I also was learning many useful skills.

An email arrived in my box about *Launch My Book*. Institute for Integrative Nutrition was offering a class to write and publish our own books.

There was always a part of me that was interested in that. I was in New York City at an Institute for Integrative Nutrition conference in November; all the new authors went on stage. I was thinking *that could be me.*

I started the class and found it to be therapeutic. I used to write my story in my head when I was unable to sleep. Remarkably, once I started writing, I was able to sleep better. All the things I had locked up in my brain over the past several years were able to spill out onto the page.

I also knew that I didn't have to write everything from scratch. The blog I had created several years ago could be part of my book. It was amazing to read what I had written right after Steve died. The writing was very genuine and real. I knew that it was much better to cut and paste those entries into the book than to rewrite it.

CHAPTER 26

I'm Going to Give It a "Tri"

IN 2004 WHILE STEVE WAS in Georgia working at a summer camp, I decided to train for a triathlon. An instructor from the gym was leading the training for the Danskin race in August in Webster. We would train two times a week with running, swimming and biking. I loved biking and didn't mind swimming, so the hardest thing would be the running. I didn't enjoy it, but figured that with training I would get more into it.

The best thing about the training was the comradery with all the other women. It also was very empowering to push myself both physically and mentally to the limit.

I remember I was really excited on the day of the race. I woke up at four a.m. to drive to Webster in order to have everything prepared for the race. Everyone who participated in the race got a computerized bracelet to put around our ankles to monitor their times.

The first event was the swim. I started swimming and realized the bracelet had fallen off in the middle of the lake. I tried to find it but soon realized it would be impossible to find and, besides, I didn't want to ruin my entire race.

I raced out of the water after the swim and told them what had happened. They told me they would give my accumulated time, but couldn't give me splits for the different events. I was upset but kept going. The biking and running went well. I got my total time, but I was disappointed that I couldn't get the breakdowns.

Overall, I was so thrilled by my accomplishment! All the hard work had paid off!

That evening I called Steve down in Georgia. I asked him if he knew what that day was. He answered that it was the trade deadline. The Red Sox had just traded Nomar Garciapara. He had totally forgotten about my triathalon. I was so deflated. It was such a huge thing for me that summer, and he was totally oblivious to it.

Fast forward eleven years. I decided that at age 50 I would do another triathlon. I wanted to prove to myself that I could still do it 11 years later.

I trained at my gym for the swim portion and practiced on my own for the other two parts. I kept on postponing signing up for the race. Part of me was still scared to get back on the bike, and the other felt not ready for the running portion.

One day Mike said to me, "Let's sign up for the triathlon. If you do the Westborough event instead of the all-women's one in Hopkinton, I will do it as well. I figured that if he could sign up at age 61, I could do it at age 50!

Earlier that spring Mike had decided to switch gyms from Planet Fitness to Boston Sports Club. I told him that BSC had reduced their rates from $59 a month to $19. He was paying $10 a month at Planet Fitness, but only doing the recumbent bike, at BSC he could do classes and use the pool.

When he joined BSC, he received a free session with a personal trainer. They talked about Mike's running in high school. Mike used to be on track and ran the mile and was second in the city for his time. Zac (his trainer) saw that Mike was very passionate about running and asked why he didn't run anymore. Mike said that he didn't because his hip and back hurt when he exerted himself too much. Zac said he should try running again, and with proper training he would be able.

Throughout the spring and early summer, Mike worked with Zac on strengthening exercises and jogging on the treadmill. He changed chiropractors and started feeling stronger. Someone from his networking group mentioned that he had run in the Senior Games in June, and said that Mike should join him. Mike decided to sign up for the mile. He hadn't run competitively since high school! Everyone said that he was crazy to run at age 61 after so many decades, but Mike was determined to do it.

Mike trained all spring. He was as excited as a little kid. In June we went with his son to Springfield for the Senior Games. Mike ran the mile, came in second, and won the silver. We were all so excited for him.

He soon learned about other races that he could compete in. He signed up in July again for the mile at the Bay State Games. This time he won the gold in his age category. His time was 7 minutes and 39 seconds.

I decided to do the triathlon because I was so inspired by Mike's determination to run again. It was really exciting practicing running on the track with him. Even though I run much slower, I was excited to be sharing this endeavor with him.

We signed up for a Sunday morning 5K training in a nearby town. The alarm went off and I was exhausted. I turned it off and said to Mike," I think I just want to sleep." At first he agreed. Then he bolted out of bed and said that we had to go. "We said we wanted to train for the running portion of the tri so let's go."

I was very glad we did. We got to the bike path. There were six other people training too. Mike ran along with me. It was 3.14 miles. The majority of the way back was a hill. I was determined not to stop. I ran the entire thing. At the end I said, "Mike, you should sprint the last leg." He bolted and then I ran faster to the end as well. I had never run that far without stopping. It felt like a huge accomplishment.

I think part of me is doing the triathlon to prove to my old gym teacher that I didn't deserve to be in a special gym class just because I couldn't do the flex arm hang. I suffered through gym classes in junior high because I was not as strong or coordinated as other kids.

I look at myself now and I see myself as an athlete. I can do so many more physically challenging activities now than I could back in school (those many years ago). In my school days they didn't offer the variety of options in gym class. If you couldn't play softball or gymnastics, you were singled out. Now kids have more options and can enjoy other activities if they can't do the traditional sports. What would my junior high have been like if I could have taken spinning or Zumba?

I am doing the triathlon to prove that I don't give up in my life. Things may be hard, but I will tri my best anyway.

CHAPTER 27

I Tried and Succeeded!

Mike and I at the Westborough Triathlon

A WEEK BEFORE THE TRIATHLON, Mike and I were going to go to a beach we love in Rhode Island. We were going to take our bikes so we could get another ride in before the race. When the alarm went off at 7:30am, we both looked at each other and said "just a few more minutes." The next thing we knew it was 8:30am.

We said to each other, "Why are we going all the way to Rhode Island? What we should do is practice for the triathlon." So we got out of bed and leisurely made breakfast and read the paper. I was afraid that we would just put it off all together and hang out all day.

After doing some errands for the event, we finally got to the lake around 1:30. The good part about delaying was that it was sunnier and warmer than it was in the morning.

We brought our bikes to the lake and had the lifeguards watch them while we swam the lake portion of the event. I felt pretty good. It was really different from swimming in the pool. The slow part was the transition from getting out of the lake to putting on my bike shoes.

The bike ride went pretty well. Mike was way in front of me, but I just kept plugging along. Finally it was time to run. Since we were just practicing for the race we decided to run together. After the last turn, I really tried to gun it. I felt pretty strong. Overall, I felt really good -- ready for the real thing the following week.

The day before the race, we had to register and pick up our packets. We both felt very anxious and punchy. We participated in an orientation which reviewed the course and some helpful hints about the upcoming event.

We went home and had a carbo- loaded dinner. We set up our bikes and our bags and went to bed early.

The day of the triathlon was beautiful, but very warm (80 degrees). Mike and I got up at 5 am to make sure we were ready. We ate a healthy breakfast, stretched, and packed our individual backpacks. We arrived at the gathering area with plenty of time to spare. We were taking out our gear; I heard Mike shout "I can't find one of my bike shoes!" He ran over to the car — no shoes; he drove home - no luck. So he brought his hybrid bike just in case he had to ride in his regular sneakers. As he was coming back to his spot, one of the volunteers asked him if he had lost his shoe. Five minutes before his age group was to go into the water, he was finally ready.

Both of our races went really well. The swimming seemed much harder than our practice run the week before. Each group was separated by type of ride, age, and sex. My wave was the 50-55 year old group. We entered as couples. We raced into the water and dove in. For the first time I didn't even notice the temperature of the water. I only noticed the waves created by all the people swimming at once. We were competing against each other, but also against the weeds! Finally, I was running to the transition point and found my bike.

I quickly laced up my bike shoes and pushed the bike up the hill to the mounting station. At first I felt a little shaky. My legs felt more tired than I had expected. Once I was on the main road though, I was fine. I knew the route very well because it was part of our regular ride. The biking portion was the highlight of the race. On one of the hills, I was behind someone going slowly, so I shouted out "On your Left" (code *for I am passing you*). I heard the woman say, "Great she is in my age group!" I was psyched to be strong enough to pass people on the hill, and that kept me going.

The run was a bit tougher. I decided to wear a camelback (a backpack for water); I figured it would be easier to wear one instead of having to reach down on the bike while I was riding. I decided to wear it for the run. As a result, the run was a lot harder because it was bulky and challenging to keep my pace. I made it back to ball field which is close to the end of the race - and saw my husband and neighbor cheering me on. I was determined and excited to finish the race. When I finished, I was tired but thrilled that I had done even better than 11 years ago!

If you don't "tri" you won't succeed in your life. So always keep trying.

Conclusion

LESSONS LEARNED

I realized that I will always have doubts and questions about my skills and life choices. I have gone through a lot over the past several years, and now I know that I can make it through.

What kept me going over the years was loving friends and family. My husband Mike has been my rock. I feel so incredibly fortunate that I was able to fall in love again.

My faith has been very important to me. Many people question God when bad things happen to them. I instead looked to God to give me strength to make it through.

My Jewish community has been a huge part of my life. They were there through the losses as well as my good times.

A valuable tool I learned at the Institute for Integrative Nutrition was about doing a gratefulness journal. One instructor recommended that we write in the early morning for a half hour without interruptions. She recommended writing about dreams and things I am grateful for. When I am down, I make sure to write in the journal to make sure I am appreciative for everything good in my life.

I hope that this book will be a way for people to see that life goes on after a set- back, whether the loss of a loved one, or even a job.

Whenever you feel down, realize that you have the strength to Bounce Back and get your life back.

While writing this book I realized that my mission is not only to help people lose weight on a diet, but also to help people gain the strength to move on after a loss —to give themselves time to heal and also permission to be happy again. That is the rainbow after the storm.

About the Author

BETH WHITMAN IS A HOLISTIC Health and Wellness coach and Founder and Owner of *Bouncing Back.* Beth lives with her husband Michael in Westborough, Massachusetts. For the majority of her career she worked within the non-profit world serving college students for nearly fifteen years. After losing both parents and her husband, she decided to switch gears to work helping others deal with grief and create a new and more purposeful life.

In her memoir, Beth weaves stories of her losses of her parents and husband with examples of how she found love again and new purpose in her life.

With the creation of her business *Bouncing Back*, Beth works with clients to *Regain their Life and not their Weight.* She works with individuals and groups teaching clients to lead a more healthful life through cooking classes, one-on-one counseling, and group classes.

This book will enable people to gain valuable lessons from their losses and have the courage to recreate their lives. Beth is available for speaking engagements as well as private consultations. For more information contact Beth at beth@bouncingback.biz or visit her website at http://www.bouncingback.biz.